Queensland's Tropical Paradise

The Great Barrier Reef
and Coastal Hinterland

Queensland's Tropical Paradise

The Great Barrier Reef and Coastal Hinterland

Alison Cotes

This edition first published in Australia in 2002 by
New Holland Publishers (Australia) Pty Ltd
Sydney · Auckland · London · Cape Town

14 Aquatic Drive Frenchs Forest NSW 2086 Australia
218 Lake Road Northcote Auckland New Zealand
86 Edgware Road London W2 2EA United Kingdom
80 McKenzie Street Cape Town 8001 South Africa

First published in 1998 as *The Great Barrier Reef: Australia's Tropical Paradise.*

Copyright © 2002 text: Alison Cotes
Copyright © 1998 maps: New Holland Publishers (Australia) Pty Ltd

All rights reserved. No part of this publication may be reproduced, stored in a retrieval system or transmitted, in any form or by any means, electronic, mechanical, photocopying, recording or otherwise, without the prior written permission of the publishers and copyright holders.

A CIP record is available from the National Library of Australia.

ISBN: 1 86436 798 9

Publishing Manager: Anouska Good
Editorial Coordinator: Jacquie Brown
Editor: Emma Wise
Design concept: Tricia McCallum
Cover design: Nanette Backhouse
Reproduction: Dot'n Line (Aust) Pty Ltd
Printer: Kyodo Printing, Singapore

2 4 6 8 10 9 7 5 3 1

Alison Cotes gratefully acknowledges the generous assistance of Tourism Queensland in gathering the material for this book.

Extract on page 12 from *The Coral Battleground* by Judith Wright reprinted with permission from HarperCollins Publishers.

All photographs courtesy of Tourism Queensland (photographer Peter Lik) except as credited below:

NHIL=New Holland Image Library **NF**=Nature Focus
t=top, b=bottom, r=right, l=left, m=main, v=vignette
Shaen Adey/NHIL: cover br, title page, pp 13t, 14m, 15, 16, 18, 19, 21 t+b, 30–1, 34 t+b, 36–7, 38m, 39, 43b, 44 t+b, 50–1t, 50b, 51b, 52–3, 56–7, 57 t+b, 59b, 60t, 61, 63b, 64–5, 72tl, 72–3, 75 t+b, 76 tl+bl, 79 t+b, 82 tl+bl, 84–5, 85br, 88t, 89, 98b, 99 tl+tr, 112tl, 118b, 119br, 138 t+b, 146b, 147tr, 151 t+b, 154b; **Bruce Elder/NHIL**: p.136t; **Lincoln Fowler**: pp 87b, 93b, 100–1, 102t, 108–9b, 114–15, 137; **Anthony Johnson/NHIL**: cover m + tr, endpapers, pp 63t, 74, 117, 120b, 121, 129, 136b; **Compliments of Lizard Island**: p.54bl; **Mike Prociv/Wetro Pics**: pp 60b, 92b; **Becca Saunders**: front cover oval inset, pp 8, 12b, 26 m+v, 28, 29 t+b, 54–5, 66b, 68–9, 102b, 120t, 139b; **Mark Spencer**: front cover inset l+r, pp 27, 88b; **Dave Watts/NF**: p.32l; **Duane Yates/NF**: pp 32–3.

cover: Whitehaven Beach, Whitsunday Islands; rainforest on Cape York; the Great Barrier Reef.
right: Sugar cane fields at Ingham.
following pages: Port Douglas.

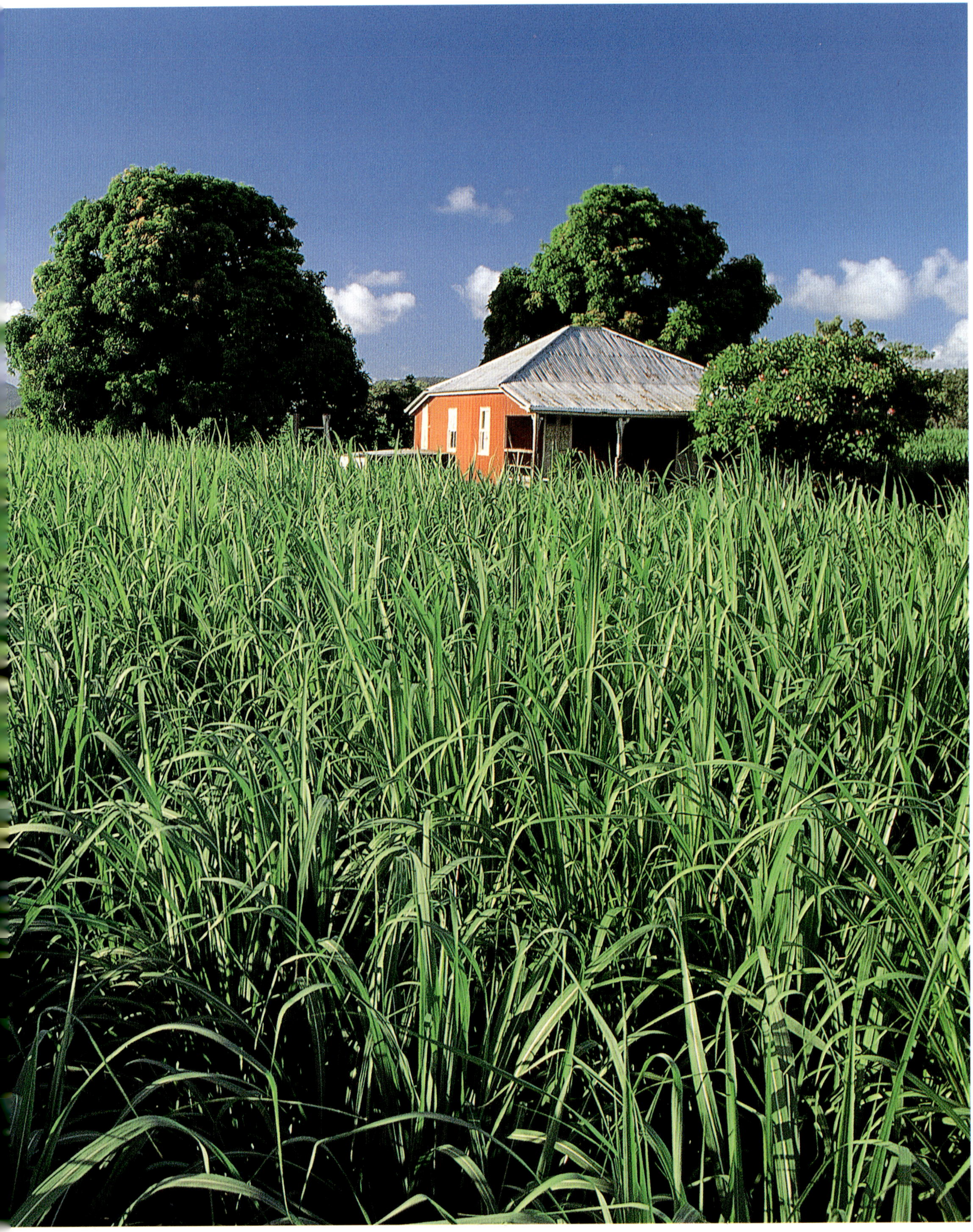

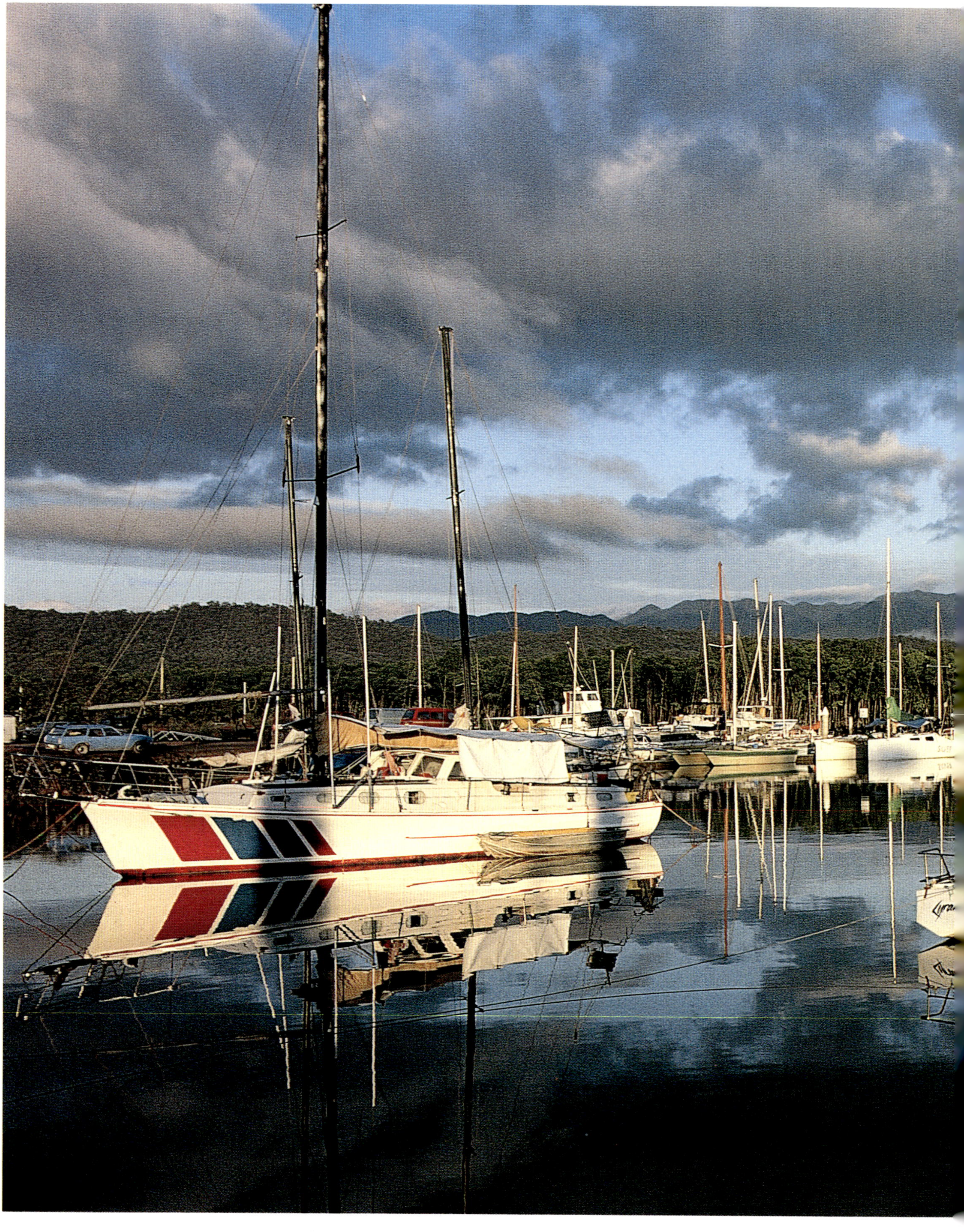

Contents

Introduction
Australia's unique tropical heritage
10

The Far North
Where the rainforest meets the reef
46

Cairns
Queensland's northern playground
68

Around Townsville
Crystal clear waters and a magnetic lifestyle
94

The Central Coast
Harvesting nature's bounty and island hopping
114

The Southern Reef
Coral cays, sugar cane, manta rays and beef
140

Index
160

above: Spectacular displays of coral, such as this one shown feeding at night, reveal the fascinating underwater world of the Reef.

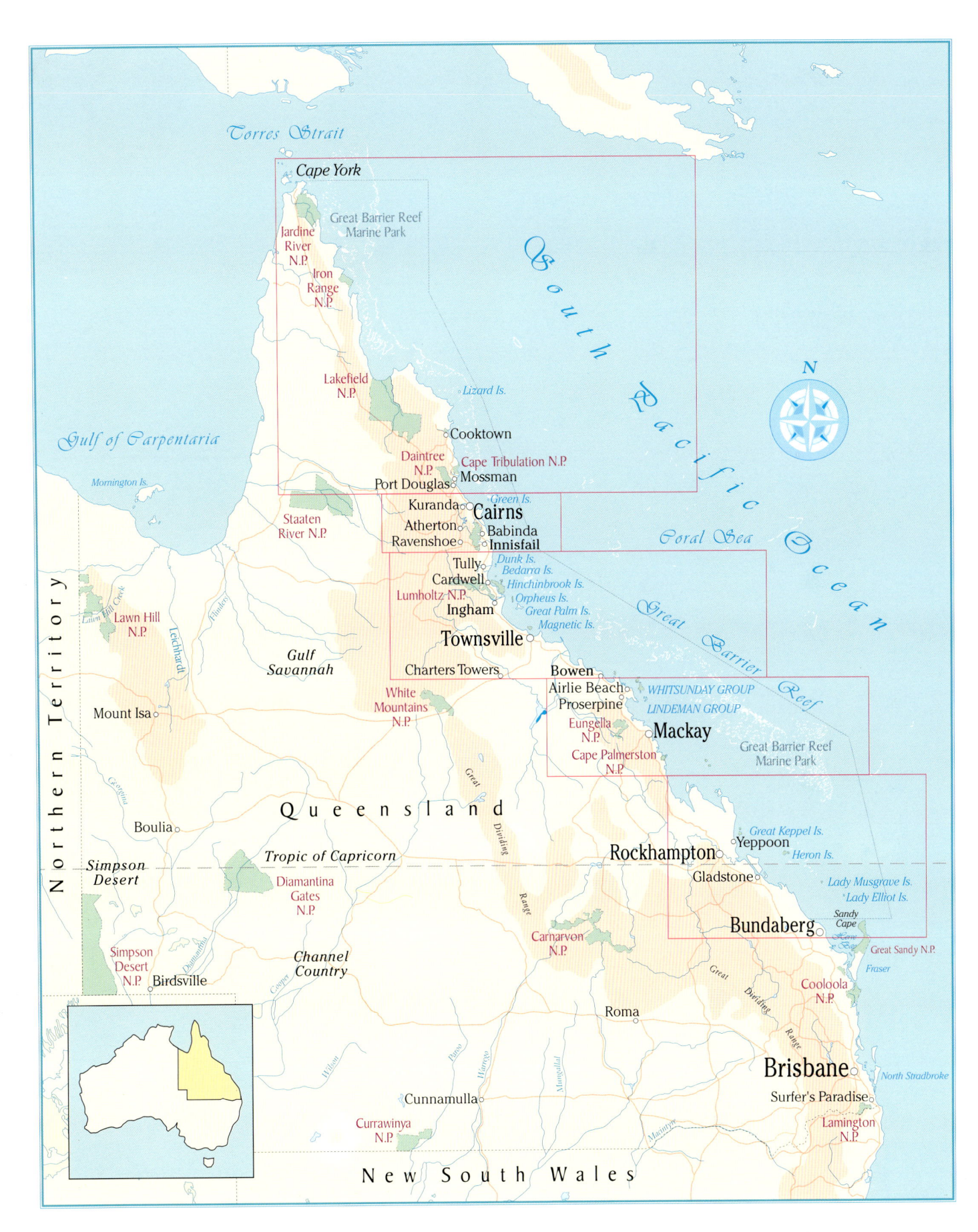

above: Map showing the regional divisions of the Great Barrier Reef, moving from north to south, as discussed in each chapter.

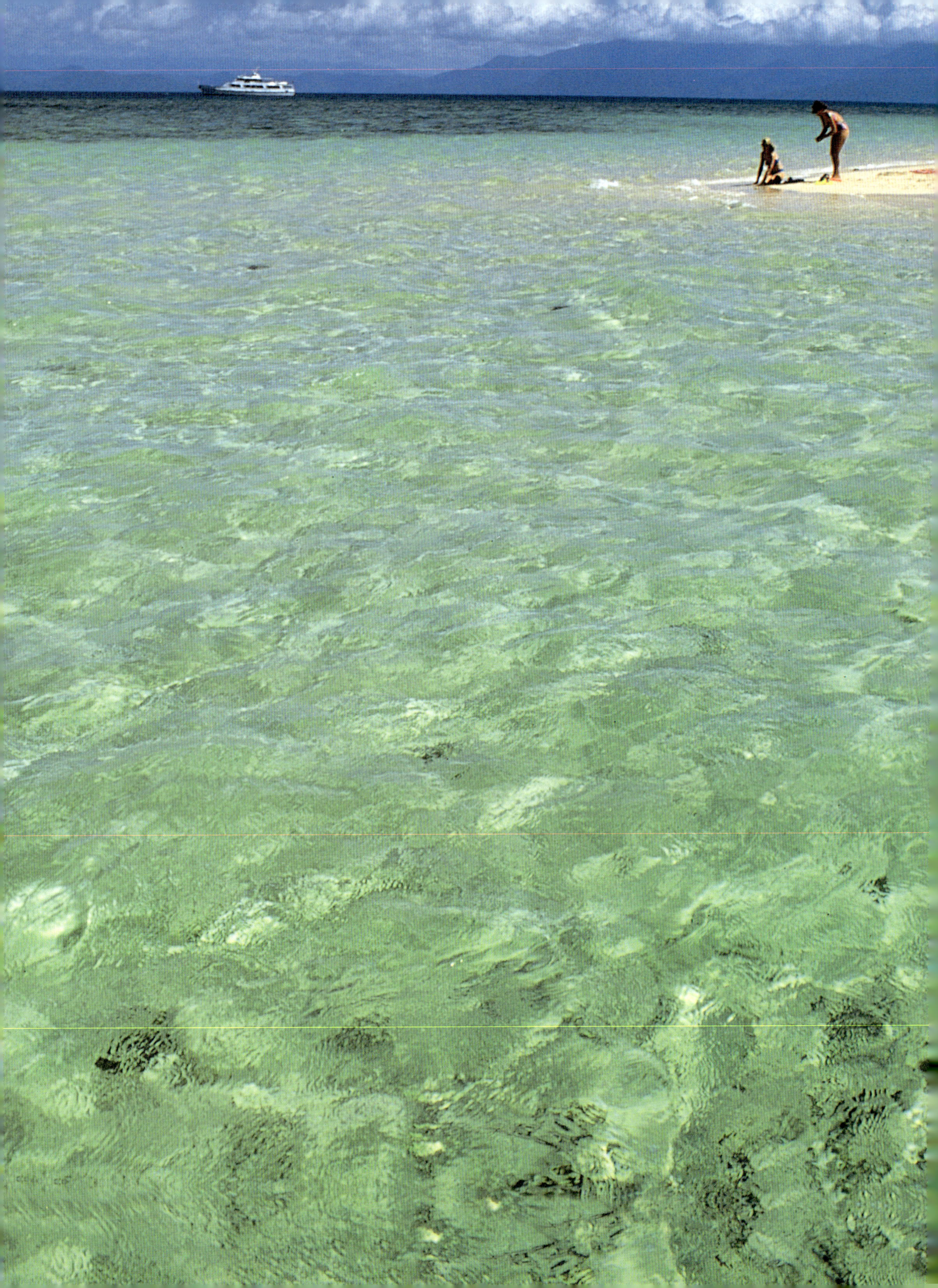

INTRODUCTION
Australia's unique tropical heritage

On a still blue summer day, with the ultramarine sea scarcely splashing the edge of the fringing reef, I was bending over a single small pool among the corals. Above it, dozens of small clams spread their velvety lips, patterned in blues and fawns, violets, red and chocolate browns, not one of them like another. In it, sea-anemones drifted long white tentacles above the clean sand and peacock-blue fishes, only inches long, darted in and out of coral branches of all shapes and colours. One blue sea star lay on the sand floor. The water was so clear that every detail of the pool's crannies and their inhabitants was vivid, and every movement could be seen through its translucence. In the centre of the pool, as if on a stage, swayed a dancing creature of crimson and yellow, rippling all over like a wind-blown shawl.

Judith Wright
The Coral Battleground

above: Riotously colourful fan coral provides a magical background for some of the Reef's many varieties of fish.
previous pages: An underwater world literally at your fingertips — holidaymakers experience the Reef first-hand on Undine Cay.

INTRODUCTION

Captain James Cook may have completely missed Sydney Harbour on his exploration of the east coast of Australia in 1770, but he couldn't miss the Great Barrier Reef. His ship, the *Endeavour*, ran aground near present-day Cooktown, and he had to drag it up the river for repairs. 'A reef such as is here spoke of is scarcely known in Europe,' he wrote in his log, which must have been the understatement of the 18th century, for the Barrier Reef is regarded as one of the natural wonders of the world and has World Heritage and Australian national park listings.

The Great Barrier Reef means different things to different people. To Captain Cook and the early European explorers it was a place fraught with danger waiting to tear their ships apart; to biologists it is a rare treasure house with many of its riches still to be explored. The abundance of big fish like black marlin and tuna attracts those interested in game fishing, while commercial fishing fleets use it as a major source of income. For some people it is simply the most beautiful place in the world to live, and for hundreds of thousands of others, it offers one of the most exotic holidays of their dreams.

Tourists come to the Barrier Reef, and the parallel coastline and hinterland, to play. They swim, snorkel, scuba dive, walk, windsurf, sunbathe, drive, eat and relax, but above all they come to marvel at the sheer magnificence of huge stretches of often untouched beaches, lush rainforest, hundreds of islands both large and small, and an exotic underwater world of unpolluted waters, forests of branching corals and millions of multicoloured fish. It is a world of magic, of fascination and of mystery.

The Great Barrier Reef is big, far too big to be appreciated in one visit. It stretches for more than 2000 kilometres off the coast of Queensland, beginning around the Tropic of Capricorn and ending in the Torres Strait which separates Cape York from Papua New Guinea. It contains thousands of individual reefs and hundreds of islands varying in size from tiny sand cays to heavily wooded drowned 'continental' islands — once part of the mainland but cut off by rising water levels after the last ice age.

above: Dunk Island caters for everyone from luxury-loving resort-dwellers to campers getting down to basics in the rainforest.

When people think of the Great Barrier Reef they tend to think island resorts, but very few of the resorts are actually on the Reef itself. The Reef can be well out to sea, especially in the more southern reaches which can be as far as 300 kilometres from the coast, with a huge 'lagoon' between the coast and the outer reef dotted with tiny reefs and islands. In the north it is much closer to the coast and the reefs and islands are much denser. Most of the islands are uninhabited but about twenty of them have commercial resorts which range from secluded sophistication to cheap hostel-style accommodation. It is also possible for visitors to camp on many of the islands.

Thousands of visitors from all over the world come to the Great Barrier Reef every year, ranging from cheerful backpackers to seekers of five-star luxury. But whether they paddle in the shallows, swim with green turtles, bag a black marlin or manage to spot the rare Bennett's tree kangaroo, they have all come for the same reason — to revel in this unique natural wonder, for nowhere else in the world can they find such an incredible combination of marine and tropical delights.

above: Hardys Reef in the Whitsundays is just one small part of the massive labyrinthine structure of the Great Barrier Reef.

A RICH HERITAGE

Most Australians, and an increasing number of overseas visitors, think that the Great Barrier Reef sounds like paradise on earth. Yet the Australian Aboriginal people, who first arrived on the mainland around 40 000 years ago (making 200 years of European settlement just a moment in time), tended not to settle on the Barrier Reef, except for a few of the larger islands such as Hinchinbrook, Whitsunday, Great Keppel and Dunk. Middens have been found on some of these islands, and in 1770 Captain James Cook, the first Englishman to explore this section of Australia's coast, recorded seeing Aborigines on the islands or in small boats.

below: The redoubtable Captain Cook was the first Englishman to chart the Reef. His statue dominates the town which bears his name.

A rich heritage – INTRODUCTION

Mainland people used dugout canoes for their forays out to the islands, whereas the island dwellers preferred to use sheets of bark stitched together with vines. They used these canoes to journey to other parts of the Reef and to the mainland for religious ceremonies as well as to spear dugongs, sharks and turtles.

An easy-going people living in an environment that gave them everything they needed, Aborigines lived off the land and had no need to create great architectural monuments. But their ancient rock art, painted mainly on the walls of caves or under overhanging ledges, is far more sophisticated than anything that was being done in Europe at the time, and their rich mythology, intricate art forms and intimate relationship with the land have only recently been appreciated by contemporary Australian society.

Lizard Island in the far north is an interesting example of the way Aboriginal people used Barrier Reef islands. For five mainland family groups it was a place where they held initiation ceremonies as well as a source of food and water. The remnants of an Aboriginal ceremonial ground can still be found at Cook's Look — the peak in the middle of the island named after the famous explorer, who in 1770 climbed it hoping for a view that would show a passage through the Reef for his patched-up ship *Endeavour*.

above: The Tjapukai Aboriginal Cultural Park is helping to keep the language and traditions of the people of the Cairns area alive.

It is possible that the death of Mary Watson, her baby and a Chinese servant, may have come about because she unknowingly strayed onto this sacred ground which seems to have been forbidden to women. Mary and her husband had set up camp on Lizard Island as a base for collecting bêche-de-mer — black sea-cucumbers, still a much-prized delicacy in China. Her diaries record that on 29 September 1881, while her husband was away on a collecting expedition, a group of ten Aborigines attacked the camp, killing one of the Chinese servants and wounding the other. Mary decided it would be safer to leave, so, taking her baby and the wounded servant, she put to sea in one of the iron pots used to boil up the bêche-de-mer, but all three died of thirst about two weeks later.

This story is particularly tragic, for when the iron pot containing the bodies was found washed up on a nearby island three months later it was half-full of rainwater. In addition, an immediate and savage reprisal was carried out against the Aborigines — about 150 people from the mainland were slaughtered, even though they almost certainly had nothing to do with the incident.

Although James Cook is credited with being the first non-Aboriginal seafarer to explore the east coast of Australia, it is possible that ships from China, Portugal and Spain arrived before he did. Colonial expansion had already spread as far as Timor, and Chinese sailors are known to have journeyed far afield in search of new food delicacies. Nevertheless, it was Cook who charted the east coast in 1770 and claimed the new land for Great Britain in the name of King George III.

Although the north-eastern coast was explored by Cook in the 18th century and Matthew Flinders in 1802, and the inside passage was charted by 1819 to become a safe and fast shipping route along the east coast, there was very little European settlement in this part of Australia, and almost none on the Great Barrier Reef itself, apart from itinerants like the Watson family. Even those settlers who flocked to Brisbane Town in the free colony of Queensland after 1842

SHIPWRECKS ON THE REEF

Captain James Cook may have been one of the first to strike trouble on the Great Barrier Reef, but he was certainly not the last. Over 1000 ships were wrecked along the Reef before 1900, including the British frigate HMS *Pandora* in 1791. This well-preserved wreck was discovered in 1977 and excavation is continuing. The liner *Quetta* came aground in 1890 with the loss of 173 lives, and in 1899 a cyclone destroyed at least 50 boats of a pearling fleet. One wreck, at Happy Bay on Long Island, is reputed to be that of a Spanish galleon, and silver coins, cutlery and even cannonballs have been recovered.

The most notorious island on the Reef for shipwrecks is also the most southerly, Lady Elliot, known as Queensland's 'shipwreck island'. It was used as a base for the bêche-de-mer industry soon after the explorer Matthew Flinders was wrecked on a nearby reef, but it was not named until 1816 when the *Lady Elliot* was wrecked there. Since then there have been regular wrecks on the island, the most famous being Ben Lexcen's *Apollo I*, which hit the island during the Brisbane to Gladstone yacht race in 1980.

INTRODUCTION - *A rich heritage*

(the first settlement in 1825 had been a penal institution) were slow to take advantage of the beauties and attractions of the Great Barrier Reef.

The first European to settle on an island was the legendary beachcomber EJ Banfield, who built a small house on Dunk Island and lived there with his wife Bertha from 1897 to 1923. They are buried in a joint grave in the island's rainforest, the stone cairn still carefully tended by the owners of the modern resort.

It wasn't until the period between the two World Wars that popular resorts were established on some of the Barrier Reef islands. Particularly after 1945, when Australians were once again able to take holidays, snorkelling and scuba diving became popular pastimes on the Reef and tourism grew steadily. By 1967 there were 250 000 visitors annually and, while the Reef had always been dear to the hearts of Queenslanders, there were very few safeguards against pollution and degradation. Many of the early tourist operators could see no further than the quick bucks that were there to be made and, by 1974, tourism had become the fourth largest industry in the State of Queensland. The Queensland Travel and Tourist Corporation was established, new resorts were built, and it seemed as if there would be nothing to stop commercial interests from taking advantage of the massive tourist trade.

Gradually, however, grave concerns began to be raised about the ecological damage that could come about through unchecked tourism, as well as from possible oil spills from the huge tankers that used the inner passage of the Barrier Reef. The water was in danger of contamination from fertiliser run-off from the mainland, the state government was threatening to drill the Reef for oil, there was large-scale removal of coral and shells, and the crown-of-thorns starfish was starting to destroy the living coral in huge quantities.

above: The rainforest meets the Reef at Cape Tribulation, possibly the most perfect place to experience the two worlds of the tropics.

An increasing realisation of the dangers motivated public attempts to preserve the vast yet delicate ecosystem from exploitation by governments and developers. Leading conservationist and poet Judith Wright was one of thousands of Australians who supported the 'Save the Barrier Reef' campaign of the late 1960s, a campaign that attracted widespread popular support and was directly responsible for a moratorium on oil drilling in the area. In 1975 the Great Barrier Marine Park was established under the administration of the Great Barrier Reef Marine Park Authority in Townsville, and in 1981 the Reef was given World Heritage listing.

Today the management of the Barrier Reef is carefully controlled. Mining, drilling for oil, removal of coral and most shells, commercial spearfishing and spearfishing with scuba gear are totally prohibited, as are all domestic animals and any kind of firearm. The Reef is now divided into a number of zones which allow different kinds of use. The General Use A Zone provides for all reasonable uses, including shipping and trawling, while General Use B Zone excludes trawling and general shipping. The Marine National Park A Zone is intended as an area where the Reef can be appreciated and enjoyed, so recreational activities are allowed here, as well as line fishing with one line and one hook per person. The Marine National Park B Zone is a 'look but don't take' area, to be preserved in its natural state, so all activities (including fishing) which remove natural resources are prohibited. Areas where the general public are not allowed are the Scientific Research Zones, where even scientists must have a permit to enter, and the Preservation Zones, where all entry is prohibited except in an emergency. Prohibited areas are clearly marked, with regular patrols carried out by rangers in planes and boats.

TRIUMPH OF NATURE

Naturalist Vincent Serventy points out that despite its name the Great Barrier Reef is not a barrier at all, or even a single wall of coral, but a great labyrinth of reefs and islands which stretches from the Tropic of Capricorn in the south to Cape York and the Torres Strait in the north.

The most extensive reef system in the world, the Great Barrier Reef is the world's largest structure made up of living organisms. It covers an area greater than the landmass of Great Britain and half the size of Texas, and a single reef may contain more species of fish than does the entire Atlantic Ocean. As the statement supporting the bid for World Heritage listing says, the Great Barrier Reef 'supports the most diverse ecosystem known to man' and 'provides some of the most spectacular scenery on earth and is of exceptional natural beauty'.

It contains 3000 individual reefs, varying in size from less than a hectare to 100 square kilometres, over 900 islands, and 69 coral cays with permanent vegetation. The life forms supported by these geological structures are even more diverse, with over 400 kinds of corals, 4000 types of clams and snails (molluscs), 1500 species of fish, and countless thousands of worms, sponges, crustaceans, and echinoderms (starfish, jellyfish and sea urchins), not to mention turtles, dugongs, whales and dolphins, and endless varieties of birds.

Geologically, the Barrier Reef was formed comparatively recently, probably only 60 000 or 70 000 years ago when the sea level stabilised after the last great ice age. The structure of the Reef is derived from a primitive life form called the marine polyp, closely related to the jellyfish. The coral polyp secretes limestone, which surrounds it with a hard exterior surface, and when the polyp dies this bony exterior remains. It is these 'skeletons' which in their billions form the Reef — new polyps live and grow on the old ones and so the Reef keeps growing.

Coral requires strict conditions for growth, such as a water temperature that does not drop below 17.5°C. This dictates a southern limit at roughly the Tropic of Capricorn. It also needs clear salty water where sunlight can penetrate, so it does not grow around river mouths or below 30 metres. This has benefits for the tourist, of course, because the best coral grows where the climate is consistently warm and where visibility is clear.

below: The clear waters around Lady Elliot Island on the southern Reef provide unsurpassed and easily accessible snorkelling and scuba diving.

INTRODUCTION – *Triumph of nature*

True coral islands, of the type popularised in the 19th century by the novelist RM Ballantyne, are low-lying coral cays where even at high tide the reef is above the water level. They have sparse vegetation but superb beaches of the purest white sand ground down from the coral by the movement of the waves. On these islands it is possible to snorkel without going more than 50 metres out from the shore. Coral cays are not geologically stable, especially at the narrower ends, and because they have little vegetation they can be badly damaged during cyclones. As they rarely have a permanent water supply, resorts built on coral cays have to provide their own water desalination plants.

Many Barrier Reef islands, however, are not made of coral at all, but are the tops of ancient mountain ranges, drowned by the rising seas thousands of years ago. They are usually very hilly and heavily wooded with volcanic soil similar to the neighbouring mainland, and over long periods of time fringing reefs have built up around some of them.

Vegetation on the islands of the Reef can range from thick rainforest on places like Dunk and Bedarra in the Family Group to nothing more than low-growing creepers on some of the uninhabited coral cays. But other cays, like Bushy Atoll off Mackay or Heron Island off Gladstone, are heavily vegetated with dense pisonia forests where seabirds flock in their thousands during the nesting season — often to the annoyance of visitors, who find that wide-brimmed hats are necessary for much more than simply protection from the sun!

Although the Great Barrier Reef lies entirely within the tropics and subtropics, there are still climatic variations between the north and the south. It is always warm, but during the Australian winter (June to August) the waters around the southern resorts like Heron and Lady Elliot islands may be too cool for comfortable swimming. During the wet season (December to March) many people desert the tropics north of Cairns because of the high rainfall and the possibility of cyclones. It is, however, worth looking at comparative rainfall charts. Cairns itself has twice as much rain in February and March than Lizard Island further north, while the areas around Rockhampton and the southern reef islands of Great Keppel, Heron and Lady Elliot have very low rainfall. Temperatures can drop to 18°C in July and August, and rise as high as 30°C in the north during January and February.

Australia has the highest incidence of skin cancer in the world, and even during the wet season when the skies are cloudy, the threat of sunburn is always present. It is essential to use 15+ sunblock at all times, wear a shady hat, and cover up with a T-shirt while swimming. Other sensible precautions are to drink copious quantities of water to guard against dehydration — a common danger in hot climates — and to wear old sneakers while walking on the Reef to avoid coral cuts.

For those who want to see the great humpback whales migrating to the Antarctic with their newborn calves, the best times are between July and October, while the turtle laying season (best observed on Heron and Lady Elliot islands) runs from November to January or February. The bird nesting season in the south usually extends from November to March, which may be a drawcard or a drawback, according to your tastes.

TYPES OF REEF

Just as there is more than one kind of island, there is more than one kind of reef. Fringing reefs develop on the underwater slopes of continental islands or along the coastline itself and, because they are the most accessible, they are also the most vulnerable to destruction through human contact. Ribbon reefs, which are mostly found in the northern sections of the Barrier Reef, are like narrow walls of coral on the edge of the continental shelf. This 'wall' is fragmented rather than continuous, and some of the gaps are large enough for ships to pass through, as Captain Cook discovered to his great relief when he was navigating these dangerous waters in 1770. Platform or patch reefs are formed when coral grows outwards in all directions from a continental shelf in a round or oval shape.

below: When you're not snorkelling, there's always the shoreline. This path through the boulders is at Nelly Bay on Magnetic Island.

Triumph of nature - INTRODUCTION

above: One of the world's last untouched wildernesses, the rainforest on Cape York Peninsula is home to literally thousands of species of plant and animal life.

A CORNUCOPIA OF ISLANDS

There are literally hundreds of islands along the 2000 kilometres of the Great Barrier Reef. Some are almost as densely inhabited as the mainland; some are totally desolate with no water or vegetation; some are ideal for rough camping; and some have accommodation ranging from permanent tents to luxury hotels.

Most people, however, stay in one of the 23 resorts which start at Lizard Island in the far north and go as far south as Lady Elliot Island just off Bundaberg. The type of resort depends entirely upon the type of holiday desired, and they are designed to suit all budgets. There are resorts for those who want to live in the fast lane, for those who crave privacy and for those who just want a basic family holiday. If a resort isn't your idea of a holiday, another way to see the Barrier Reef is to hire a yacht, moor offshore and live on board while visiting the islands for snorkelling or birdwatching.

The far north

Lizard Island is not only the archetypal reef island, at 240 kilometres from Cairns it is also the most remote, with most visitors arriving there by light plane. The island is tiny but boasts 24 picture-book beaches, probably the clearest water on the Reef, and superb coral so close to shore that you can swim out to the Clam Gardens — where the giant clams are over 200 years old — in five minutes. It is also the jumping-off point for boat trips to the world-famous Cod Hole where giant potato cod, Maori wrasse and moray eels can be handfed. Serious game fishing is organised from here too, with people coming from all around the world from August to November to catch the renowned black marlin. Chefs at the resort often serve other kinds of fish brought in that day by successful guests. The Lizard Island Resort is one of the most exclusive on the Reef, taking a maximum of 60 guests, and European and British royalty are among its regular visitors. It is a high volcanic island, only 18 kilometres from the outer Reef, covered in grasslands and woodlands and home to many different varieties of seabirds as well as the great monitor lizards. Lizard Island is a national park, and there is also a small camping ground.

Islands around Cairns

Because Cairns is the largest mainland tourist centre for the Reef, the islands closest to it are mainly visited by day-trippers, although there are also resorts for those who want to stay overnight. While Green Island has a fine resort, it is best known as a daytrippers' paradise (people who prefer privacy might consider it hell). About 250 000 people a year make the 45-minute trip from Cairns in order to take a glass-bottomed boat out to see the coral, swim in the clear waters, or indulge themselves in the many trendy food and clothing shops on the island which cater for bulk tourism. There is also Marineland Melanesia which has crocodiles, sharks and other terrifying marine monsters in display pools, with coral and smaller tropical fish in tanks, and a

above: Instant snorkelling on Lady Elliot Island — wade out knee-deep, flip face-down, and you're right among the coral and the fish.

collection of Melanesian artefacts. This is not really the place for snorkelling or scuba diving as much of the coral close to the island has been destroyed by the crown-of-thorns starfish. For serious diving it is better to continue on the catamaran to tiny Michaelmas Cay where 30 000 seabirds nest in the summer months, and where the reef hugs the beaches for at least 10 kilometres.

The Family Islands

Offshore from Tully (reputed to be the wettest town in Australia) and Mission Beach, lies a group of eight islands which are among the most idyllic on the Reef. The daddy of them all, Dunk Island (its Aboriginal name is Coonanglebah), is where the legendary beachcomber E J Banfield settled in 1897 — the first European to take up residence on the Great Barrier Reef. The island now has a large very popular resort, with an emphasis on family holidays — there are two swimming pools, three restaurants and special activities twice a day for children. It is the place for active sports like parasailing, beach volleyball, archery and waterskiing, and there is also a small golf course. The beaches are shallow and sandy without much coral but they are ideal for beachcombing, and the walks through the rainforest are a way to escape from the crowds at the resort bar.

Bedarra Island, known to the local Aborigines as Biagurra, is closed to daytrippers, and its one remaining resort, Bedarra Bay, is as close to perfection as you're likely to find. This is the place for the totally self-indulgent. Its list of 'NOs' is its most positive selling point — no children under sixteen, no daytrippers, no tour groups, no package deals, no 'activities', no entertainment, no extras once you've paid your (very high) daily tariff. The food is all one would expect and more, and when couples on their first or second honeymoon finally emerge from their luxurious chalets, they can order a packed

below: Not even summer storms can eclipse the beauty of Missionary Bay on Hinchinbrook Island, the world's biggest island national park.

above: From Dunk Island, known as the father of the Family Islands, it's possible to see all the other members of the clan.

hamper with a bottle or two of superior champagne or chardonnay and go off in a dinghy to one of the island's many secluded beaches. And if they tell the staff where they're going, other guests with similar inclinations will be delicately warned not to intrude on that particular beach.

Hinchinbrook Island

Hinchinbrook is so huge that when Captain Cook sailed past he did not realise it was an island at all. Its 39 000 hectares make it possibly the world's biggest island national

INTRODUCTION - *A cornucopia of islands*

park, and most of it is untouched wilderness. It contains lush rainforest, long sandy beaches and some magnificent mangrove forests at Missionary Bay where a boardwalk has been constructed for a close-up view. While there is a small resort at the northern tip, camping is permitted anywhere on the island. You won't find outstanding swimming and diving here, but it is one of the best islands on the Reef for bushwalking.

The Palm Islands

Eight of the 10 islands in this group are reserved as Aboriginal land and permission must be obtained to visit them. Orpheus Island, however, is a national park and visitors may either camp there or stay in the small exclusive resort which takes a maximum of 74 guests. The beaches here are among the best on the Reef, and not far offshore are some good bommies (from the Aboriginal word 'bombora' meaning submerged reef of rocks, in this case, coral outcrops) with excellent coral.

Magnetic Island

Magnetic Island, just off the coast of Townsville, is a mere 20 minutes away from the mainland by launch, and is the only worthwhile holiday island as far as the locals, who affectionately refer to it as 'Maggie', are concerned. It has a very different feel from the resort islands, as it contains a number of suburbs and small townships and concentrates on low-budget and middle-market accommodation rather than exclusive resorts and hotels. The most popular way to get around Maggie is to hire one of the cheap-and-cheerful Mini Mokes. There are excellent beaches, very good coral in some of the bays, and self-guided reef walks for low-tide activities. Magnetic Island also has Australia's largest koala colony — these furry marsupials are not native to the island, but were introduced early this century and have bred very successfully in the wild. Horse and camel riding are popular activities, and at Geoffrey Beach one of the resorts has regular cane toad races — not a pretty sight, as the cane toad is one of the ugliest and most destructive amphibians in Australia, but a fantastic drawcard for lively and enthusiastic tourists.

The Whitsunday Islands

There are 70 islands in this group, all reached from Airlie Beach on the mainland. They are drowned mountain tops rather than genuine reef islands, although some of them have fine fringing reefs. Daydream, Hayman, Hook, South Molle, Long Island, Hamilton Island, Lindeman and Palm Bay are the most accessible and contain the most popular resorts, but many visitors prefer to indulge in a little island hopping, staying at a different resort every couple of nights.

As Captain Cook said in his journal in 1770, 'the whole passage may be considered as one safe harbour, exclusive of the small bays and coves which abound on each side, where ships may lie as in a basin.' The protected waters mean that the Whitsunday region is the charter yacht capital of Australia, and one very popular way of seeing it is to charter a bareboat (skipper, crew and provisions not provided) and sail around the islands, mooring at whatever spot takes your fancy. People who are nervous about their sailing skills sometimes prefer to book a cruise, and there are several options available — some tours visit a number of islands in a single day, some drop passengers off at just one island for the whole day, while others are 'go-as-you-please' charters which keep away from the resort islands and go to the remote uninhabited areas. On the whole, although the diving in the Whitsundays is good, tidal variations mean the beaches aren't outstanding.

Of the islands in the Whitsunday group, Hamilton is the biggest and caters for mass tourism; Long Island is for the young and noisy; Daydream is geared towards families;

below: For a combination of spectacular natural scenery and all the comforts of an elegant resort, Hamilton Island is the place to go.

INTRODUCTION - *A cornucopia of islands*

right: Sometimes the most remote atolls are the most beautiful. Bushy Atoll, which provides a perfect escape from the crowds, can be reached either by private yacht or by regular seaplane excursions from Mackay.

below: Snorkellers can find plenty to excite them just a few metres offshore, but serious scuba divers on Heron Island prefer to take a boat out to the deep reefs to dive the famous bommies.

Hayman provides expensive luxury; Hook offers a low-key resort for backpackers as well as some of the best diving and snorkelling in the Whitsunday Islands; South Molle is unsophisticated but fun; and Lindeman Island is the more middle-of-the-road alternative.

Southern Barrier Reef Islands

Brampton Island, reached by a 40-minute launch trip or a 10-minute flight from Mackay, has lovely beaches and good offshore snorkelling. The wreck of the SS *Geelong* off the adjoining Carlisle Island is a popular snorkelling spot, but there's not much on these islands for scuba divers, who have to take boat trips to the outer Reef.

'I got wrecked on Great Keppel', the slogan used to say, and for a number of years this island was more famous for its wet T-shirt competitions than for the magnificence of its beaches, which are, however, as good as you will find. Although things have calmed down in the last couple of years, Great Keppel still has a reputation for being a place for the young and restless. It's cheap and cheerful, and definitely not for urban sophisticates!

For many visitors, Heron Island is the best of them all. 'Just a drop in the ocean', they call it, and you can walk right around it in half an hour. This tiny coral cay on the Tropic of Capricorn has incomparable beaches and some of the finest snorkelling and diving in the world. It is also home to the beautiful Barrier Reef herons and thousands of mutton birds which make a noise like crying babies. No daytrippers are allowed, and at the middle-market resort you are expected to make up your own entertainment, although marine biologists from the University of Queensland's Research Station pop over most nights to guide the turtle-watchers (Heron Island is an important hatching ground for green turtles) and to give talks on the ecology of the Reef.

The southernmost island on the Reef is Lady Elliot, and it too is a coral cay. This means that the island is actually part of the reef and, as soon as the water is deep enough to swim in, you're right among the coral. Turtles nest here in the summer season, as do thousands of birds, and it is one of the few islands where it's possible to scuba dive from the shore. Accommodation in the resort ranges from safari tents to motel-like units facing the lagoon, democratic rather than luxurious. Food is plentiful and good, not gourmet quality, but as people come here to dive rather than be pampered there are no complaints.

The Outer Reef

Although this is where you find the best diving, there are no resorts on the outer Reef itself. There are day excursions from mainland centres like Cape Tribulation, Port Douglas, Cairns, Townsville, Airlie Beach, Yeppoon, Bundaberg, Mackay and Gladstone, and many tour companies have mooring rights and permanent pontoons from which beginning snorkellers and divers can see the best parts of the Reef without getting into trouble and without damaging the coral on the Reef itself. The trips are usually on swift catamarans or launches, although yacht cruises are offered too. In some cases seaplanes will take swimmers and snorkellers out to places like Bushy Atoll off Mackay — people susceptible to sea-sickness often prefer this to two- or three-hour launch trips.

AN ISLAND FOR EVERY TASTE

HIGH CLASS, EXCLUSIVE AND EXPENSIVE: Lizard, Bedarra, Orpheus, Hayman

SERIOUS DIVING: Lizard, Hook, Orpheus, Heron, Lady Elliot

GREAT BEACHES: Lizard, Great Keppel, Heron

CHEAP AND CHEERFUL: Fitzroy, Magnetic, Lady Elliot

SUPERCHARGED: Great Keppel, Contiki Resort on Long Island, Hamilton

FAMILY HOLIDAYS: Fitzroy, Dunk, Hinchinbrook, Daydream, South Molle, Lindeman, Brampton, Great Keppel, Magnetic

MASS MARKET: Dunk, Great Keppel, Hamilton, South Molle

RAINFOREST COVER: Bedarra, Dunk, Hinchinbrook

CORAL CAYS: Green, Heron, Lady Elliot

DAYTRIPPING: Fitzroy, Green, Dunk, Hinchinbrook, Magnetic, Daydream, Hamilton, Lindeman, Great Keppel

WATER SPORTS: Fitzroy, Dunk, Long

FISHING: Lizard, Dunk, Hinchinbrook, Orpheus, Daydream, South Molle

ADULTS ONLY: Lizard, Bedarra, Orpheus

CAMPING: Lizard, Fitzroy, Dunk, Hinchinbrook, Orpheus, Magnetic, Hook, Long, Lindeman, Carlisle, Great Keppel and many of the uninhabited islands without resorts

WILDLIFE: Lizard, Magnetic, Hinchinbrook, Heron

LIFE ABOVE AND BELOW WATER

Corals, fish, cowries, cone shells, feather stars, turtles, sea urchins and dolphins — the Great Barrier Reef is home to teeming millions of creatures from the tiny coral polyp to the massive manta ray.

Corals

Until 250 years ago coral was commonly believed to be a form of plant life, and even today many people who look at the soft colourful waving fronds find it hard to believe that they are actually made up of tiny living creatures. The coral polyp is one of the wonders of nature — one of the world's tiniest animals is the architect and builder of our planet's greatest organic structure.

There are two basic types of coral — hard and soft — but each is a form of the coral polyp. The polyp is similar to the anemone, a soft cylinder of tissue closed at one end, with a mouth surrounded by tiny tentacles at the other. Corals may be tiny (one 15-tonne colony was found to contain 30 million individual polyps), but they are savage carnivores that are relentless in their quest for food, using their stinging tentacles to trap smaller forms of animal life and sometimes even small fish. Because individual polyps in coral colonies are organically connected to one another, food caught and digested by one polyp becomes part of the entire colony's nutritional system.

A symbiotic relationship exists between most reef-building corals and microscopic single-celled plants called zooxanthellae which live inside the cell tissue of the polyps. These plants live off the carbon dioxide produced by the coral and the sun's energy, and in return produce oxygen and sugars which help boost the growth rate of the coral. They are also instrumental in providing the brilliant colours of the coral, although pigments in the outer layers of the coral tissue also contribute to the variety of colours. When the polyps die, so does the colour — white coral is dead coral.

Hard corals secrete a rigid skeleton of limestone within which they live, withdrawing during the day and coming out at night to feed. They grow in many different ways: by branching out in a tree form, by growing in layers on top of older dead coral structures, or by extending new polyps around the edge of the colony. Staghorn, brain, plate and mushroom corals are the most easily identifiable.

Soft corals have no lime skeletons, and their colonies are made up of thousands or millions of polyps connected to each other by fleshy tissue. These are the corals that, with their waving foliage and vivid colours, look like plants, and often form thick carpet-like structures over the massive reefs formed by hard corals that have died.

There is an extremely delicate ecological balance between hard and soft corals — recent studies have shown

left: So soft and fluid are their movements, it's hard to believe these dendrophylliid corals are actually animals rather than plants.

opposite: In a riot of rainbow colours, the delicate branches of fan corals wave in the currents like leaves in the breeze.

Life above and below water - INTRODUCTION

INTRODUCTION – *Life above and below water*

that soft corals release toxic substances into the water that can retard the growth of hard corals and eventually kill them. The fact that soft corals have a shorter life span and can be severely damaged during storms is the only reason that the balance is kept intact.

Although some corals reproduce by budding off from the parent colony, most reproduce sexually in a spectacular mass display of spawning that takes place two or three times a year, usually around the full moons in October and November. Because most corals are hermaphrodites, both sperm and eggs are produced in a technicolour explosion and unite in the water. They drift for a few days until they settle and form new colonies of their own.

Strangely enough, very few corals are attacked by the fish which abound on the Great Barrier Reef. About half of the soft corals are poisonous to fish, the taste of many of the others is unappealing, and some corals have tiny needles of limestone which protect the delicate polyps. The main enemies of coral are the crown-of-thorns starfish, which has destroyed whole coral colonies, and parrotfish when present in large numbers. Apart from that, the worst enemies of the coral are human beings, who can wreak havoc either through careless diving, deliberately breaking or harvesting the coral, or inadvertently through chemical run-off from agricultural areas.

above: The famous Clam Gardens, off Lizard Island, are home to hundreds of ancient giant clams, each uniquely patterned and coloured.

Shells

There are more than 4000 mollusc varieties that produce shells on the Great Barrier Reef but, in order to save the marine environment from damage, shell collecting is limited and the regulations strictly enforced. Unrestricted collecting can have serious effects — it has been suggested that one reason for the proliferation of the crown-of-thorns starfish is that the triton shell, which feeds on the young starfish, has been depleted by over-zealous collectors.

Limited shell collecting, which means not more than five examples of any one shell type in a 28-day period, is allowed only in General Use Zones A and B, which are not the areas where most of the island resorts are found. So a 'look but don't take' policy operates, which means that visitors who admire the cowries, spider shells, volutes, strombs or cones will have to buy them at tourist shops if they want to take the memory home as anything more than a photograph. Cone shells contain a particularly venomous poison and should never be picked up.

Molluscs

Members of the mollusc family include oysters, clams, cowries, cone shells, squid, octopus, and nudibranchs (meaning simply 'naked lungs'). Some of the giant clams have shells that weigh 200 kilograms and are up to one metre in length. The fleshy muscles, which shut tight and have given rise to unsubstantiated horror stories about humans being trapped and drowned, are coloured with brilliant indigos, emerald greens and deep purples, and no two are the same. Nudibranchs are snails without shells and their colours are, if possible, even more amazing than those of the fish. Their patterns range from stripes of red, orange, white and purple to splodges of black and white edged with gold, and orange plumes and horns flaring from their backs; many people consider them the most enchanting form of marine life on the Reef.

Echinoderms

Feather stars, with as many as 200 arms, are the most primitive of this group, and look more like plants than animals. Starfish can be seen all over the Reef, with colours ranging from vivid blue, although some are patterned like red-tiled mosaics. Sea urchins are most often seen in the form of 'sea eggs', the fragile, delicately patterned ball that remains when the spines have fallen off after the creature has died. The villain of this group is the crown-of-thorns starfish, one of the few life forms to attack and kill coral polyps. Since 1960 these creatures have multiplied to such an extent that they have destroyed large sections of the Reef. Fortunately, they tend to concentrate in specific areas rather than being widely spread. No natural predator has been found to destroy them, so to stop the damage they cause they have to be physically removed — as this is not possible over such a large area, ecologists have been relieved to find that numbers seem to have stabilised in the last 10 years or so.

Another common echinoderm on the Reef is the sea cucumber, also known as trepang or bêche-de-mer. These harmless uglies can be found all over the Reef, their soft leathery bodies squirting sea water and sand from each end when they are picked up. They are regarded as a great delicacy in Asia, and they became one of Australia's earliest export industries in the 1840s.

Fish

Banded humbug, bass, barramundi, barracuda, beaked coral fish, black kingfish, black marlin, black-tipped rock cod, black-saddled toby fish, butter bream — and those are just the Bs! The Great Barrier Reef is home to more than 2000 species of fish including everything from tiny gobies, which weigh less than a gram, to black marlin which have weighed in at 1000 kilograms. Most of the fish, however, are quite small — well under a kilogram — and very few are harmful. Even the long sleek reef sharks which strike fear into the hearts of novice snorkellers as they glide past aren't usually interested in human beings; they are so well fed that they don't need to attack.

The sheer beauty of reef fish is their immediate attraction. There's the bright orange of the coral cod spotted improbably in blue, the buttercup-yellow angelfish with its bright blue snout and green fins and tail, the broad black and white stripes of the banded humbug, the orange clown fish with its

above: A pair of orange anemonefish peep curiously from their coral shelter. If you come too close, they'll quickly disappear.

white stripes edged in black, and the pastel blues and pinks of the fairy basset. Amorphous manta rays undulate gracefully through the water like sheets blowing on a washing line, giant potato cod come up to mumble food out of divers' hands, translucent cuttlefish swim backwards when disturbed, their beady eyes fixed suspiciously on the potential enemy, and the cleaner wrasse nibbles parasites, dead scales and fungal matter off the scales of larger fish, and even darts in and out of their mouths to clean their teeth.

below: This magnificent coral cod may seem too beautiful to eat, but its sweet flesh makes it a best-seller in the fish markets.

INTRODUCTION - *Life above and below water*

Crustaceans

Hermit crabs spend their lives ashore rather than in the sea, and can actually drown if they are thrown into deep water by well-meaning tourists. Ghost crabs or sand crabs, considered a real delicacy, are beach scavengers, but there are other crabs that live on the Reef itself, either as swimmers or staying tucked into the coral.

Turtles

The Great Barrier Reef is one of the most important sea turtle habitats in the world, and six of the world's seven recognised species are found in the area. Although they were once heavily harvested for their meat or their shells, all turtles are now totally protected, except that Aborigines and Torres Strait Islanders living in traditional communities may hunt them for food.

Most people come into contact with turtles while scuba diving or snorkelling (swimming alongside a green turtle is one of life's joys), but if you come in the right season you can also watch them dig nests and lay eggs on Lady Elliot or Heron islands, or at Mon Repos on the mainland near Bundaberg — three important nesting sites for loggerhead and green turtles. It is important to make no noise and use no bright lights while watching the nesting.

The turtle nesting season occurs between November and March, when sometimes hundreds of female turtles crawl slowly up the beach at night, leaving tracks in the sand up to a metre wide. They dig a clumsy hole with their

Life above and below water - INTRODUCTION

DANGERS ON THE BARRIER REEF

SHARKS: Reef sharks are harmless and seldom attack human beings but, as all predators are attracted by blood, it is better not to swim with open cuts or wounds.

SNAKES: Although sea snakes have an extremely poisonous venom which can cause instant death, they rarely attack human beings.

SHELLS: The cone shell, with its fatal sting, should never be touched. It is safer not to pick up any shells at all.

CORALS: Coral cuts can become infected very easily, and should be washed and treated with strong disinfectant. Always wear old shoes when walking on the Reef.

JELLYFISH: The sting of the box jellyfish, found in coastal waters north of Rockhampton during the summer months, can bring about cardiac arrest and inflict savage scars. Never swim in coastal waters during the summer, unless it is in a jellyfish-proof enclosure. Most Reef islands are safe, however, as 'box jellies' never go more than eight kilometres out to sea. Other kinds of jellyfish also inflict a painful sting. If stung, keep calm and apply household vinegar to the affected area. Many resorts have containers of vinegar positioned on popular beaches.

FISH: Never handle fish while swimming, some have spines that cause nasty cuts and others are poisonous. The most dangerous of all is the heavily camouflaged bottom-dwelling stonefish with large dorsal spines that can penetrate light shoes. It prefers to live among coral rubble or weeds, so when swimming always watch where you put your hands and feet.

STINGRAYS: These can be found in shallow coastal areas but the chances of being stung are remote as they are timid creatures and avoid human contact.

BLUE-RINGED OCTOPUS: The only poisonous octopus of the Great Barrier Reef, and its bite is deadly. It is easily identified by electric blue rings which appear when it is disturbed. Keep well away from this creature — bites result in respiratory arrest and it is crucial that artificial respiration is applied at once.

above: An exhausted green turtle makes her way back to the ocean after laying a clutch of eggs in the sand on Heron Island.

flippers, lay a clutch of eggs (about 50 for a flatback and up to 120 for a loggerhead) then cover it with sand and retreat back to the water. They will return a number of times during the season to lay more eggs, but then may take a break for several years.

Once hatched, the babies make their own way down to the sea, but very few of them survive. Those that do remain in the outer ocean for up to 50 years, and very little is known of their life. They mate at sea, and although females come back to land to lay their eggs, the males never set flipper on land again.

INTRODUCTION - *Life above and below water*

Mammals

Great humpback whales can often be seen in August and September as they slowly make their way down the coast from their northern breeding grounds to the colder waters of the Antarctic. Whale watching (which is strictly controlled by rangers) is now one of Queensland's most popular tourist attractions.

Dolphins are also common in the region and can often be seen catching a free ride on the waves made by launches on their way to the outer Reef. Snorkellers and scuba divers have reported being accompanied on their excursions by these charming creatures who seem to enjoy playing even more than human beings.

The Great Barrier Reef is one of the largest dugong habitats in the world. As an endangered species, dugongs are protected and may not be hunted by anyone except Aboriginal and Torres Strait Islanders, for whom they have traditionally been an important food supply. These gentle creatures may have generated the ancient stories of mermaids, although up close their fatty faces are cute rather than gorgeous.

above: The humpback whale, while slow, is particularly acrobatic, perhaps because of its exceptionally long pectoral fins.

right: Dugongs often graze in shallow meadows of seagrass, their backs sometimes scarred from fights with other dugongs.

Life above and below water - **INTRODUCTION**

INTRODUCTION - *Life above and below water*

Birds

The abundance of food and the safety of the Barrier Reef islands, most of which are free from predators, make this area a very attractive one for roosting and nesting. Most islands on the Reef, therefore, are a birdwatchers' paradise, with over 200 species of seabirds and water birds having been recorded. During the summer months, however, it is possible to lose your enthusiasm for mutton-birds and noddies. Most seabirds nest on the ground, but the noisy noddies nest in the pisonia trees of the southern cays and have been cursed by many a tourist for causing sleepless nights. An estimated 100 000 of them inhabit Heron Island during the nesting period, and when the chicks fall out of the ill-constructed nests, as they often do, the parents leave them to their fate.

above: A remarkable private conservatory only 25 kilometres from Mackay nurtures many magnificent specimens of orchids like this one.

top: Pied oystercatchers in their thousands live on the islands of the Reef, where food is plentiful and predators are few.

Mutton-birds, or wedge-tailed shearwaters, are the only birds that nest in burrows in the sand, and they can be as much of a nuisance as the noddy chicks. Mutton-birds are very community minded and squawk and groan en masse, often sounding like human beings in anguish!

Other birds on the southern islands include terns, reef herons, egrets, doves and oystercatchers. Tiny silvereyes, cheeky olive-green birds which invade tables at some resorts, have even learned to lift the lids off sugar bowls. Gulls are common, of course, and, as they prey on the chicks of other birds, are universally detested and visitors are asked not to feed them.

Further north there is an even greater variety. The uninhabited Michaelmas Cay, about 40 kilometres north-east of Cairns, is one of Australia's most important seabird nesting colonies, and many cruises and charter boats regularly include a stop during the nesting season to see the six species that breed there, in numbers up to 30 000. Lizard Island, far to the north, is home to 40 different species of bird, including egrets, herons, terns, sea eagles, sunbirds, pigeons, plovers, bee-eaters and kingfishers.

The best way to observe island birds is through binoculars, and it is imperative that visitors avoid nesting sites because, if disturbed, parents have been known to desert their chicks and leave them to the mercy of predators.

Island flora

From mangrove swamps to she-oaks, from low woods to dense rainforest, there is a wide variety of vegetation on the islands of the Barrier Reef, with the volcanic islands providing a much more diverse range of trees and plants than the lightly wooded sand or coral cays.

A typical Great Barrier Reef sand cay is thickly covered with pisonia trees. These softwoods can grow up to 30 metres in height, producing sticky seeds in summer which become attached to birds' feathers and thereby carried across to other islands. Sometimes the birds' wings become so encrusted with the seeds that they are no longer able to fly and simply

Life above and below water - INTRODUCTION

above: Lindeman Island is remarkable for its variety of grasses and ancient ferns as well as for the beauty of its beaches.

fall to the ground and die. Tragic as this may seem to the soft-hearted, it is part of the natural cycle of death and rebirth, for the bodies of the dead birds add nutrients to the sandy soil on coral cays, thus providing a perfect food source for new trees. Other common trees on coral cays are she-oaks which make a soft soughing sound as the wind blows through them, and the hardy pandanus palm with a large knobbly fruit traditionally used by Aborigines as a valuable food source.

Mangroves are another common feature of many Barrier Reef islands. One of the very few plants that actually thrive in salt water, mangroves tend to grow in unstable mud flats, and their extensive root systems provide a breeding ground for many fish, shellfish and crabs and even the dreaded box jellyfish. One of the most important mangrove swamps is on Hinchinbrook Island, where an observation boardwalk has been built through the swamp.

Vegetation on the continental islands is similar to that of the mainland. Lizard, Bedarra, Dunk and Hinchinbrook Islands have large areas of lush rainforest, consisting of trees such as native nutmegs, tamarinds and turpentines, with exotic native orchids nestling shyly in the undergrowth. Continental islands such as Magnetic Island are covered with open eucalypt forests of bloodwood, stringybark and grey ironbark. Paperbarks are also common, and hoop pines, cedars, blue gums and tulip oaks abound, while grass trees, one of the most ancient forms of vegetation, can also be found on the continental islands.

Serious hikers often take the two- or three-day hike around Hinchinbrook Island on the Thorsborne Trail which meanders through some of the most beautiful and accessible rain-forest on the Reef, although the less intrepid may find the five-kilometre self-guided walk to Machusla Cove and North Shepherd Beach energetic enough.

The coastal fringe

There is much more to north Queensland and the Great Barrier Reef than the islands. The coastal fringe also offers striking scenery — the far north in particular is famous as the spectacular region where rainforest meets the reef.

Although there is good rainforest to be seen on some of the continental islands, nothing can compare with the great sweeps of wet tropical jungle north of Cairns. The rainforest at Cape Tribulation is, at 10 million years old, the oldest rainforest on earth. This is another World Heritage-listed site, embracing the greatest diversity of unique flora and fauna on earth. Only a few places in the world meet the four criteria for World Heritage listing: outstanding examples of major stages in the earth's evolutionary history, continuing biological evolution, exceptional beauty, and habitat for threatened species. As David Attenborough says, the Cape Tribulation rainforest is 'one of the most breathtakingly wild areas in the world; unbelievably beautiful, unbelievably interesting. There are birds, mammals and plants there that are unique'.

The coastal fringe - INTRODUCTION

In a world where forests continue to be cut down at an alarming rate, North Queensland's primeval Wet Tropics World Heritage area has been protected by its relative isolation. Now, however, with more than 2 000 000 visitors a year, the fragile ecology of the region is at risk, so a Wet Tropics Management Authority has been set up to provide an infrastructure that will work in close conjunction with tourist operators, allowing as many tourists as possible to visit the area while protecting it from too much intrusion. Most tourist resorts organise rainforest experiences, or link up with private operators who will take visitors on guided ecologically sensitive tours ranging from short walks to three- or four-day safaris along carefully constructed walking tracks. Night-time spotlight tours are a wonderful way to see the nocturnal inhabitants of the forest.

In the depths of the rainforest amazing Curtain Fig trees send roots down from their branches to strangle everything that grows beneath them, and primitive flowering plants that originated in the forests of Gondwana bloom beside ancient ferns and mosses which have been around since the age of the dinosaurs. There are colonies of bats, including the tube-nosed bat; rare lizards such as the Boyd's forest dragon; the potentially dangerous cassowary, a huge flightless bird; tree kangaroos which can climb to great heights to obtain the particular leaves they like to eat; the bizarre little platypus which can be found in remote waterholes; striped possums; at least 58 frog species and 327 bird species; and of course the reptile that everyone comes to see, the estuarine crocodile.

Croc-spotting is a popular tourist activity in the Daintree River, especially since the dramatic fatal attack on the local postmistress in 1985. The same incident illustrates why crocodiles are less popular with locals who see them as a danger to livestock and children. In any case, crocodile numbers are well down in spite of being a protected species since 1974 and there are usually more cruise boats than nasty reptiles in the river these days. The best way to see crocodiles is actually in one of the many crocodile parks in the region, which offer opportunities to see the reptiles close up in perfect safety. Some parks breed crocodiles for their skins, or for their meat, which is tender and juicy with a subtle fish-like flavour. Crocodile meat now features on the menus of most of the best 'bush tucker' restaurants.

below: David Attenborough has described the Cape Tribulation National Park as one of the world's most breathtaking wild areas.

Holidaying on the Reef

Although most of the Great Barrier Reef and much of the rainforest adjoining the Queensland coastline has either been designated national park or given World Heritage status, tourism is probably the most important industry in the area, and government departments and private operators work together ensuring visitors of a wide variety of experiences while limiting damage to the sensitive environment.

Accommodation

Lush scenery and a wide range of activities are the main reasons people come to north Queensland, but where they stay is also important — camping on an uninhabited island may be the best way to see nature in its purest and simplest form, but some people prefer not to accomodate themselves in anything less than absolute luxury. Resorts, hotels, backpacker hostels and camping areas offer the widest possible choice and, as well as five-star hotels in the Sheraton and Hilton chains, there are also superb resorts specialising in eco-tourism, surrounded by untouched rainforest or the pure beauty of unpolluted turquoise waters and dazzling sand, but with every luxury of civilisation. Visitors to Silky Oaks Lodge at Mossman, for example, stay in airconditioned chalets surrounded by jungle or overlooking the magnificent Mossman River as it tumbles its way down from the Gorge.

Coastal centres like Cairns and Townsville have extensive tourist accommodation, and many resorts have tree houses, free-standing bures, cabanas and even safari tents in a wide price range. Most of the architecture is now much more

below: In the most fashionable resorts the decor often echoes the tropical surroundings, like here in the Torresian Resort at Port Douglas.

Holidaying on the reef - INTRODUCTION

above: On Magnetic Island, off Townsville, low-budget backpackers enjoy the same beauties of sea and sky as the big spenders do.

environmentally sensitive than it used to be, with extensive use of cane, bamboo and natural fabrics giving a tropical feel to many of the resorts. During the Australian school holidays in December and January, the last half of April, the first half of July and the last half of September, most resorts are fully booked and may charge higher prices, so beware.

Outdoor types as well as those whose love of natural beauty is greater than their budgets may prefer to pitch a tent in one of the wide variety of camping spots available. Some islands have properly set up campsites with ablution blocks and washing facilities, others allow you to camp cheaply on an island but still join in the fun of the resort night-life, while others have nothing but pit toilets and limited fresh water. Many of the islands are national parks, but camping is still allowed on some of them as long as you have a permit from the Queensland National Parks and Wildlife Service, and strict regulations are in force. These regulations include no domestic animals of any kind (including horses); total protection of all plants, animals and natural features — which means nothing may be removed; no firearms, machetes or other weapons; no electric generators; no burying of rubbish — take it out with you; and a ban on open fires.

INTRODUCTION – *Holidaying on the reef*

Fishing

No licences or permits are required for amateur fishing in Queensland waters and, although fishing is prohibited in certain zones of the Great Barrier Reef, there are plenty of areas where it is allowed, not to mention the joys of coastal and freshwater fishing on the mainland. Maps of free-fishing zones are readily available from the Great Barrier Reef Marine Park Authority, and all resorts and mainland cities also have detailed information.

On the mainland, it is possible to catch barramundi and other fish in dams like Tinaroo and Copperlode. In the mangrove estuaries of the coastal regions bream, whiting and barramundi occur in large numbers, and this is where the celebrated 'muddie', or Queensland mud crab, is also found. Flathead congregate on the edges of sandbanks, under fallen trees or in creek mouths.

After an hour or so snorkelling or scuba diving, the tender-hearted may find it impossible ever to eat a parrotfish, red emperor, butterfly cod, or coral trout again, but their beauty doesn't deter serious anglers, for the flesh of these and other reef fish has a delicate melt-in-your-mouth texture that cannot be surpassed. Most reef fish are covered by strictly enforced bag limits.

The outer Barrier Reef is heaven on earth for anyone interested in big-game fishing, and many island resorts, especially Lizard, organise regular deep-sea excursions to catch marlin, tuna, kingfish and sailfish. Ocean-going vessels can also be charted from major coastal centres like Cairns, Port Douglas, Townsville and Airlie Beach.

above: Summertime — the fish are jumping at Bargara Beach at Bundaberg, where fishermen's dreams come true.

Holidaying on the reef - INTRODUCTION

Boating

They say if you can drive a car you can skipper your own bareboat — a popular pastime around the Whitsunday Islands. The waters here are completely safe, as they are guarded by the Reef itself, and even people with no sailing experience soon find themselves exploring uninhabited islands, discovering their own special dive sites and even catching their own dinner. If you prefer to take it a little easier you can hire a sail guide to make the important decisions about where to go and when while you snorkel, relax on archetypal deserted islands or just take a snooze on deck. Power launches, houseboats, tall ships and square riggers can also be chartered, and luxury extended cruises are available as well.

Diving and snorkelling

Even in the cooler regions of the Barrier Reef it is possible to dive all year round at southern islands like Heron and Lady Elliot; the prime diving period, however, is between May and December, before the real summer heat sets in. While some of the best diving and snorkelling is to be had off the outer Reef, accessible only by charter boat, on some coral cays it is possible to walk straight off the beach into the middle of a wonderland of coral.

You don't have to be an experienced diver to see some of the most dramatic underwater landscapes in the world — if you can swim a little, you can snorkel. Skim across gardens of coral; swim alongside a green turtle; discover a school of manta rays on the bottom of a bay, stacked up on

above: As their boat waits to take them back to shore, snorkellers off Undine Cay explore the treasures of an underwater Aladdin's Cave.

above: On Hamilton Island, one of the most popular pastimes is sailing colourful catamarans like this. When they're all out at sea at once, the scene is a cheerful collage of rainbow colours.

left: The good life begins where the sea meets the shore in a harmony of blue and white on Great Keppel Island. A beach rendezvous marks the beginning of another adventurous day.

41

INTRODUCTION - *Holidaying on the reef*

top of each other like pancakes; and, around the time of the full moon in November, experience what one diver has called underwater fireworks when the annual coral spawning takes place, releasing millions of multicoloured eggs in a technicolour snowstorm.

above: A reefweld, such as this one in the Whitsundays, allows boats to anchor on the Reef without damaging the coral.

For the best experiences, of course, scuba diving allows you to go deeper below the surface and come face to face with some of the friendly monsters of the region — moray eels, manta rays and huge potato cod, some of which are so friendly they'll literally eat out of your hand. Scuba divers can explore the great bommies, drift diving and freewheeling with the current, and experience some of the best wall diving in the world. Some operators and resorts offer eco-diving excursions, where divers are accompanied by marine ecologists and reef guides who explain the complex life forms of the Reef. There are also hundreds of wrecks along the reef and the coast that supply brilliant diving opportunities, with bright corals and thousands of fish to delight the eye even if there are no gold doubloons left to be discovered.

You don't have to be a previously qualified diver to do all this — if you are medically fit you can learn to dive in less than a week, and most resorts and tour operators provide diving instruction for beginners. The accident rate on the Reef is the lowest in the world because of the clear shallow waters and the high safety standards required by the Queensland Government.

Other kinds of reef viewing

Even people who can't swim or are afraid of water can experience the reef by joining in guided reef walks on most of the coral cay resorts, or by taking a trip in a glass-bottomed boat or a semi-submersible. The Yellow Submarine on Heron Island is very popular with non-swimmers, and in

Holidaying on the reef - INTRODUCTION

the nesting season turtles often swim alongside it, coming almost face to face with the people sitting safe and dry inside. Semi-submersibles go much deeper than is possible for most snorkellers and having a ride on one of these is a good way to explore the underwater wonders if the weather isn't perfect for swimming.

Water sports

For some people, a holiday wouldn't be worth having without water sports, and both the Reef and the coast offer a wide variety of activities — sailboards, catamarans, water-skis, aqua bikes, windsurfers, paddle skis, jet skis, motor boats, paragliders, sea kayaks, and that's just on the ocean. For mainland water sports, try whitewater rafting on a number of rivers — the Tully, Barron, Mulgrave and North Johnstone (Grade 5 rapids) are the most accessible, with packages offering added attractions like balloon flights, bungee jumping, helicopter flights or, for the less intrepid, just drifting down the quieter stretches.

Land sports

Archery, ballooning, birdwatching, cycling, horse or camel trekking, fossicking, golfing, hang-gliding, parachuting, and even bungee jumping for the young and fit — these are just some of the land sports available not only on the coast, but on many of the Reef islands as well. And there is always the attraction of bushwalking, with many self-guided trails in national parks, guided bushwalks through the rainforest or longer safaris which can take up to a week.

above: The long unpopulated beaches of the Capricorn International Resort at Yeppoon are perfect for a leisurely horse or camel ride.

below: Whitewater rafting down the Tully River provides serious thrill seekers with all the excitement they could possibly ask for.

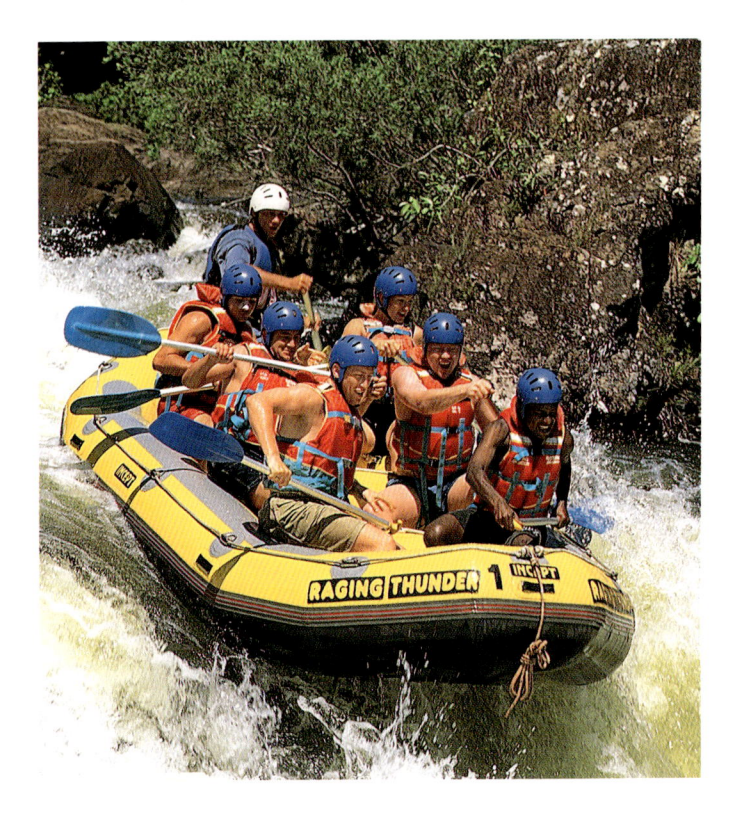

INTRODUCTION – *Holidaying on the reef*

left: The Tjapukai Aboriginal Cultural Park in Cairns gives visitors an insight to the traditional way of life of Australia's earliest inhabitants.

Exploring Aboriginal culture

Many Aboriginal people are now proud to share their rich heritage with visitors, and a large number of tours, cultural exhibitions and bush experiences are offered in places as far apart as Cape York and Rockhampton. Because Aboriginal and Torres Strait Islander sites are protected by law, permission is needed to visit them, but most tour operators have the appropriate permits.

- The Pajinka Wilderness Lodge at Cape York is in a remote wilderness at the northernmost point of mainland Australia. Field trips are available with local tribal elders showing visitors the delights of bush tucker and the mysteries of bush medicine.
- Kuku-Yalangi Dreamtime Walks offer a chance to walk with local Aboriginal guides trough the Mossman Gorge, north of Cairns, and learn about Dreamtime legends and aspects of traditional Aboriginal culture.
- Hazel Douglas's Native Guide Safaris, which also operate out of Mossman, take tourists on full-day four-wheel-drive tours through the Daintree National Park, giving both a European and Aboriginal perspective on the area.
- The Dreamtime Cultural Centre located in Rockhampton is a focus for Aboriginal and Torres Strait Islander people to share their heritage.
- The Tjapukai Aboriginal Cultural Park outside Cairns is an ambitious complex with a Creation Theatre, a History Theatre, a Magic Space, Dance Theatre and Cultural Village.
- The Rainforestation at Kuranda outside Cairns offers the Dreamtime Walk along the Rainbow Serpent as well as spear and boomerang practice, and the Pamagirri Aboriginal Dancers provide a glimpse into the ancient tradition of the corroboree.
- In Cairns itself there are a number of tours to Aboriginal sites available, many of them run by Aboriginal people. Aboriginal Tribal Tours offers tours to Aboriginal communities and also has retail outlets for local artefacts.

Spotting Australian wildlife

The most natural way to see Australian wildlife is, of course, in the wild. However, because many of the animals are very shy or come out only at night, quite often the best chance the casual tourist has to see koalas, platypuses and other unique creatures is in special reserves or wildlife parks.

- Townsville's Town Common is 10 000 hectares of wetlands where brolgas, magpie geese and other waterbirds abound, as well as dingoes and wallabies. There are well-signposted walking tracks and a number of 'hides' for viewing the lagoons and bird life, as well as vehicle access.
- At Mount Spec National Park near Townsville even daytrippers have a good chance of seeing golden bowerbirds and the Macleay honeyeater, as well as kookaburras, green ringtail possums and wallabies.
- When the Capricorn International Resort was constructed, 10 000 hectares of wetlands were left for brolgas, geese, swans and thousands of other birds to catch fish, mate, nest and rear their young. Guided tours are available for guests as well as casual visitors.
- Edward River Crocodile Farm, south of Cairns, run by the Pormpuraau Aboriginal Community, is the oldest and largest in the country.
- Koorana Crocodile Farm near Rockhampton, winner of many tourism awards, has a restaurant where the reptile appears on the menu in a number of guises. There is also a shop selling products made from the skin.

left: Traditional Aboriginal food, or bush tucker, is becoming increasingly popular. Wattle seeds, wild plums and native myrtle are now used widely in mainstream cooking.

- Magnetic Island off the coast of Townsville is one of the best places to spot koalas in the wild. While not native to the island, a very successful colony has been established and walkers on the track up to the World War II forts off Horseshoe Bay Road are usually guaranteed a good look. At Horseshoe Bay itself there is a Koala Park Oasis where they are much easier to find.
- Along the Daintree River thousands of fruit bats hang upside down like torn umbrellas on trees.
- Tiny bentwing bats have lived for hundreds of years in Olsens Capricorn Caverns and the Cammoo Caves north of Rockhampton. Tours are available, either self-guided or with a leader.
- The platypus is so timid and hard to catch that it is rare even to find one in captivity, but at Broken River in the Eungella National Park there is a quiet bend in the river where, before dawn and at sunset, seven or eight of the elusive animals may be seen feeding.
- Dunk Island is the place to see the mighty blue-winged Ulysses butterfly in the wild, but there is a much greater variety at the Australian Butterfly Sanctuary at Kuranda, inland from Cairns, where up to 2000 individual insects of 14 different species flutter through the dappled foliage. There is also a museum which exhibits butterfly specimens from around the world.
- Fourteen kilometres south-east of Bundaberg, at a beach called Mon Repos, sea turtles nest in the dunes from November to February, hatchlings emerging from January to March. The Turtle Information Station provides regular briefings on this important rookery as well as guided turtle spotting excursions.
- Turtles can also be spotted from the resorts on Heron and Lady Elliot islands, and on the uninhabited islands of North West, Wreck and Hoskyn.

left: The glorious Ulysses butterfly, symbol of Dunk Island, is one of hundreds of colourful species native to northern Queensland.

- The Kuranda Wildlife Noctarium is an excellent place for those who have neither the time nor the inclination to tiptoe through the rainforest in the dark for a glimpse of sugar gliders, possums, flying foxes, wallabies, bandicoots, echidnas and about a dozen other species.
- Cooberrie Park near Yeppoon, and Billabong Sanctuary at Townsville, are two of the better wildlife parks where experienced rangers provide fascinating information on a wide variety of birds and animals.
- At the Rainforest Habitat on the Port Douglas road, animals, birds and reptiles coexist in a habitat which is as close as possible to their natural surroundings. There is also an excellent restaurant where you can breakfast in the rainforest on local delicacies.

Other special attractions

The Great Barrier Reef Wonderland at Townsville is one of the best managed and presented tourist attractions in Australia, with a walk-through aquarium where elderly people, those with a disability, non-swimmers and small children have a chance to see sharks, moray eels, gropers and bull rays swimming over their heads, and to view the brightly coloured tropical fish that divers or snorkellers experience. There's also a giant Omnimax Theatre and the Museum of Tropical Queensland.

The Kuranda Experience is a special package operating out of Cairns that takes you first to the new Tjapukai Aboriginal Cultural Park near the Skyrail terminal, where people from the local Djabugay and Yirrukandji communities tell the story of their 40 000-year history through traditional music and dance, hi-tech films and computer graphics. Visitors then take the Skyrail, a gondola cableway, up the mountain in a glide above the rainforest canopy with two stops at specially built nature stations. After time at leisure in the village of Kuranda with river cruises, animal sanctuaries and craft markets available, the Kuranda scenic railway, unchanged in 100 years, takes you back down the range through 15 tunnels and glorious rainforest via the rugged terrain and wild waterfalls of the Barron Gorge.

left: From behind the bars at the Billabong Sanctuary in Townsville, visitors can view this potential killer safely.

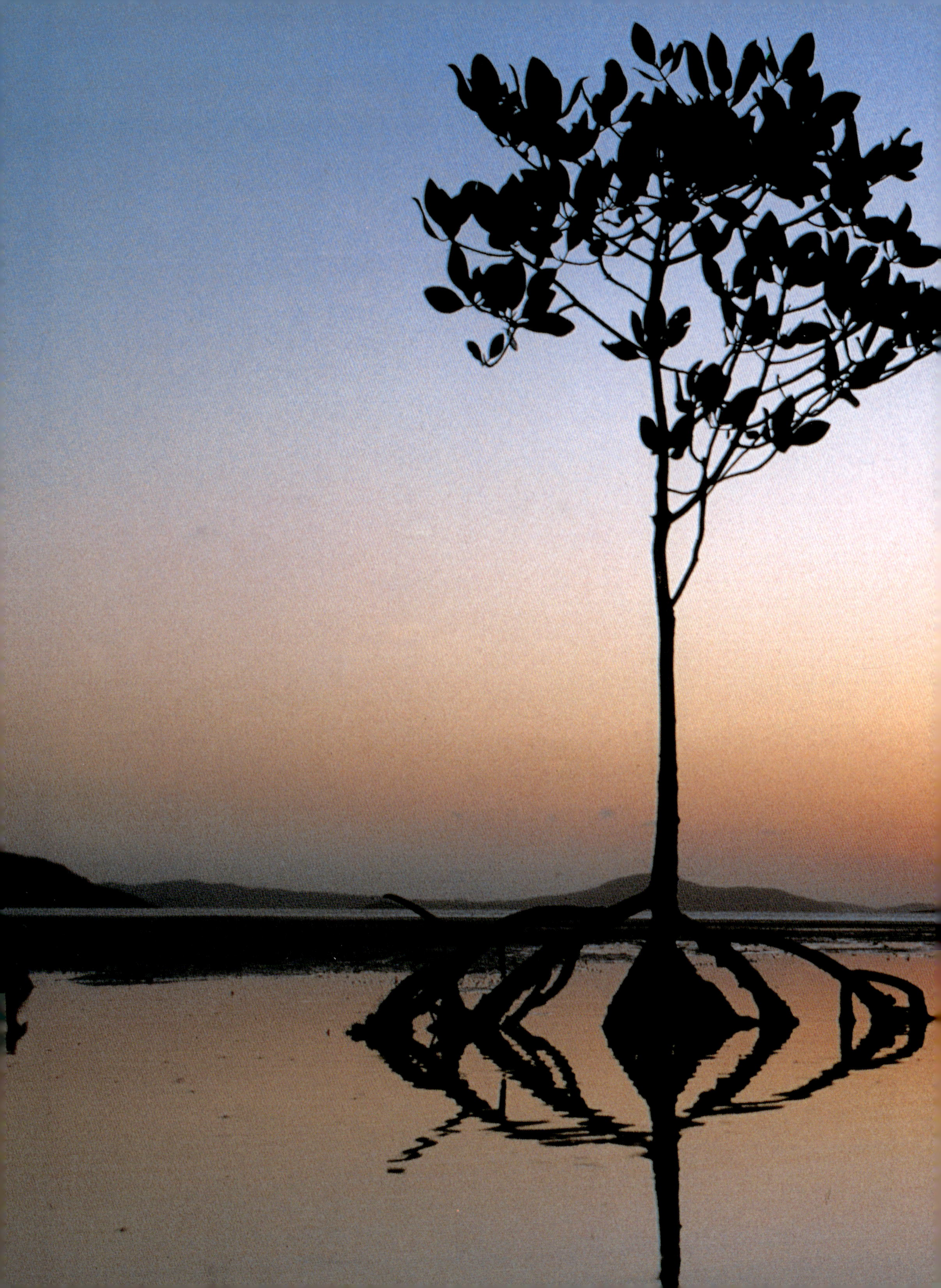

THE FAR NORTH
Where the rainforest meets the reef

To the north-east of Cairns stretches the glittering Coral Sea where some of the most remote and beautiful islands of the Great Barrier Reef stud the waters like brilliant sapphires thrown carelessly on crumpled turquoise velvet. This is the exotic world of the remote tropics, of islands like Lizard where utter luxury is combined with a feeling of isolation and adventure. Food and other supplies arrive once a fortnight by barge, and the eight-seater planes that take visitors there, while perfectly safe, still provide an exciting frisson of danger.

Lizard Island is the northernmost resort on the Barrier Reef. Although the tourist stretch ends here, serious explorers can still visit some of the uninhabited islands further north, either in a hired yacht or by booking a passage on one of the two cruise ships which provide a regular service from Cairns to Thursday Island in the Torres Strait. These boats also call in at Cape York, the northernmost tip of Australia, where drinking a glass of champagne on the beach at sunrise is a unique experience.

It is, however, the coastline north of Cairns that provides the most accessible adventures for visitors who want to recapture the pioneer spirit without taking too many risks. From the luxury of Silky Oaks Lodge at Mossman, where individual chalets nestle in the middle of the rainforest overlooking the tempestuous Mossman River, to the challenging drive through untouched World Heritage landscapes in the Daintree and Cape Tribulation area up to Cooktown (named after Australia's most famous European explorer), northern Queensland provides a range of experiences for thrill seekers and placid nature-lovers alike. This is the area where the rainforest really does meet the reef, and where the best of both worlds is there for the taking.

opposite: All the ingredients of a tropical paradise are here at Palm Cove, north of Cairns.
previous pages: Double the beauty as trees at Cape York form a mirror image of themselves in the water.

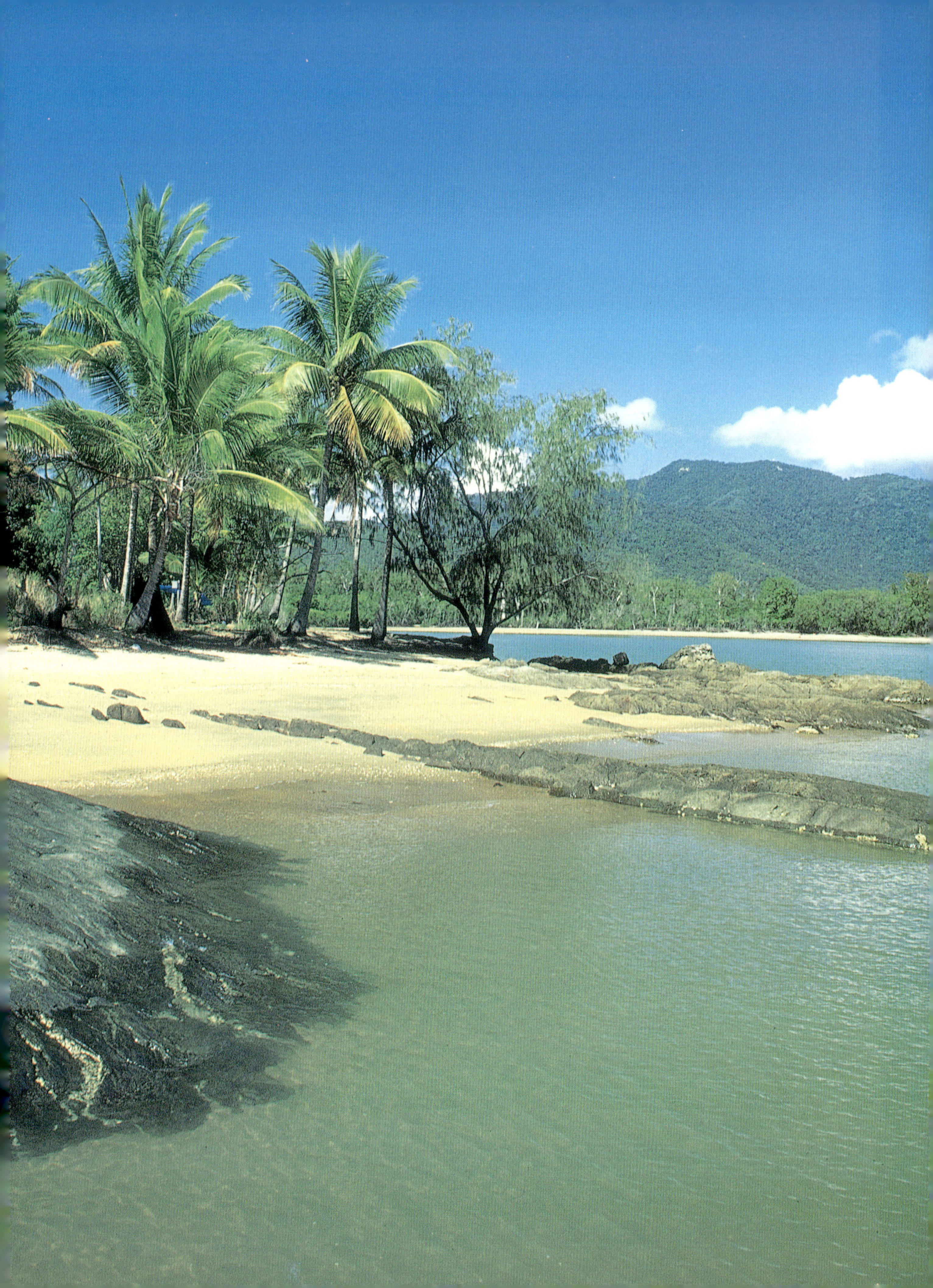

THE FAR NORTH - *Cape York*

Cape York - THE FAR NORTH

above: At Cape York, the shoreline, forest and ocean form an image like a great sweep from a painter's brush.

left: The world's your oyster, especially if you live on Cape York Peninsula like this cheerful young boy from Seisia.

opposite bottom: They're having great fun, but these swimmers first made sure the creek was a crocodile-free zone.

following pages: The coastal people of the Torres Strait are more at home in small motor boats than in cars.

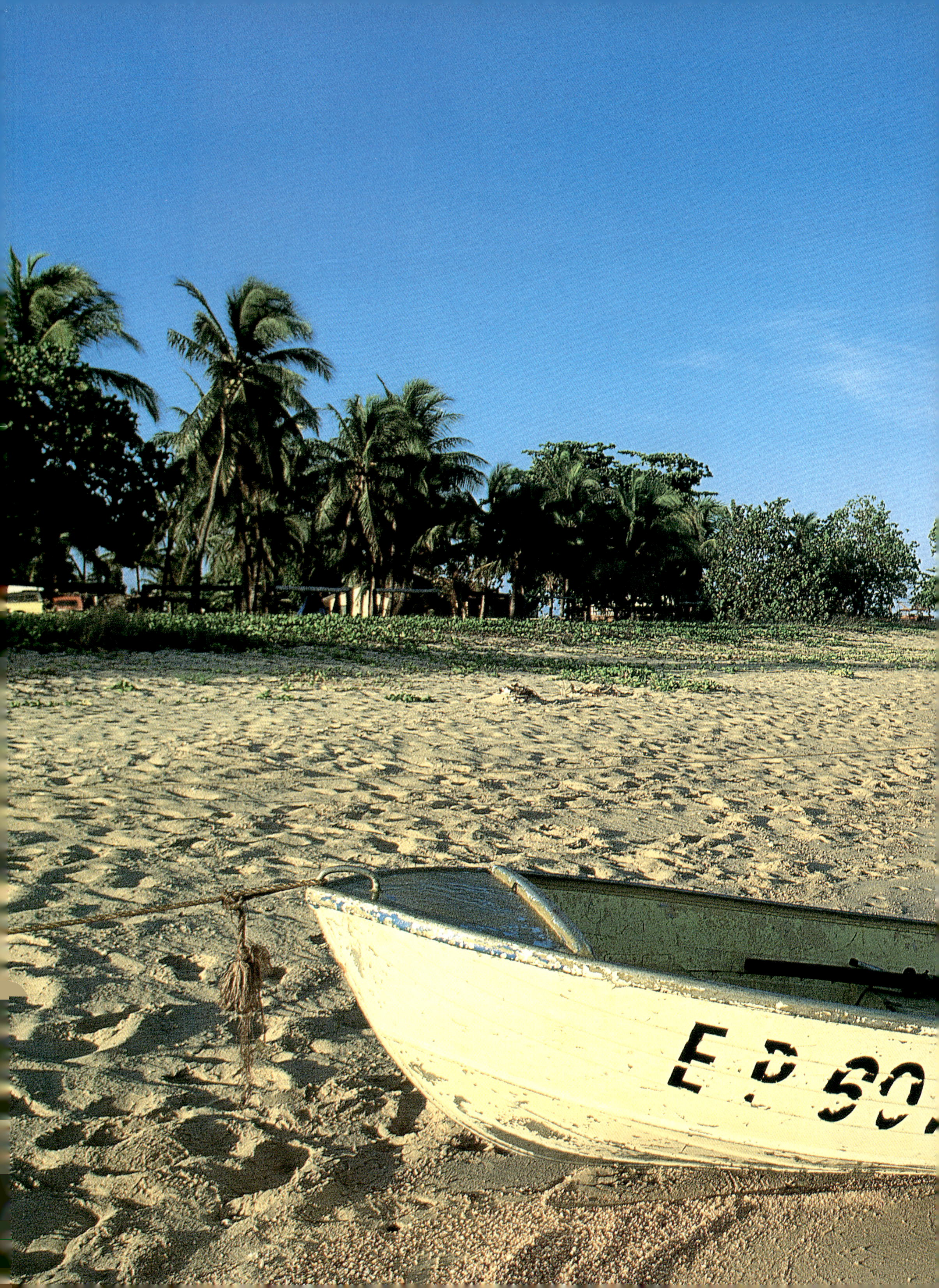

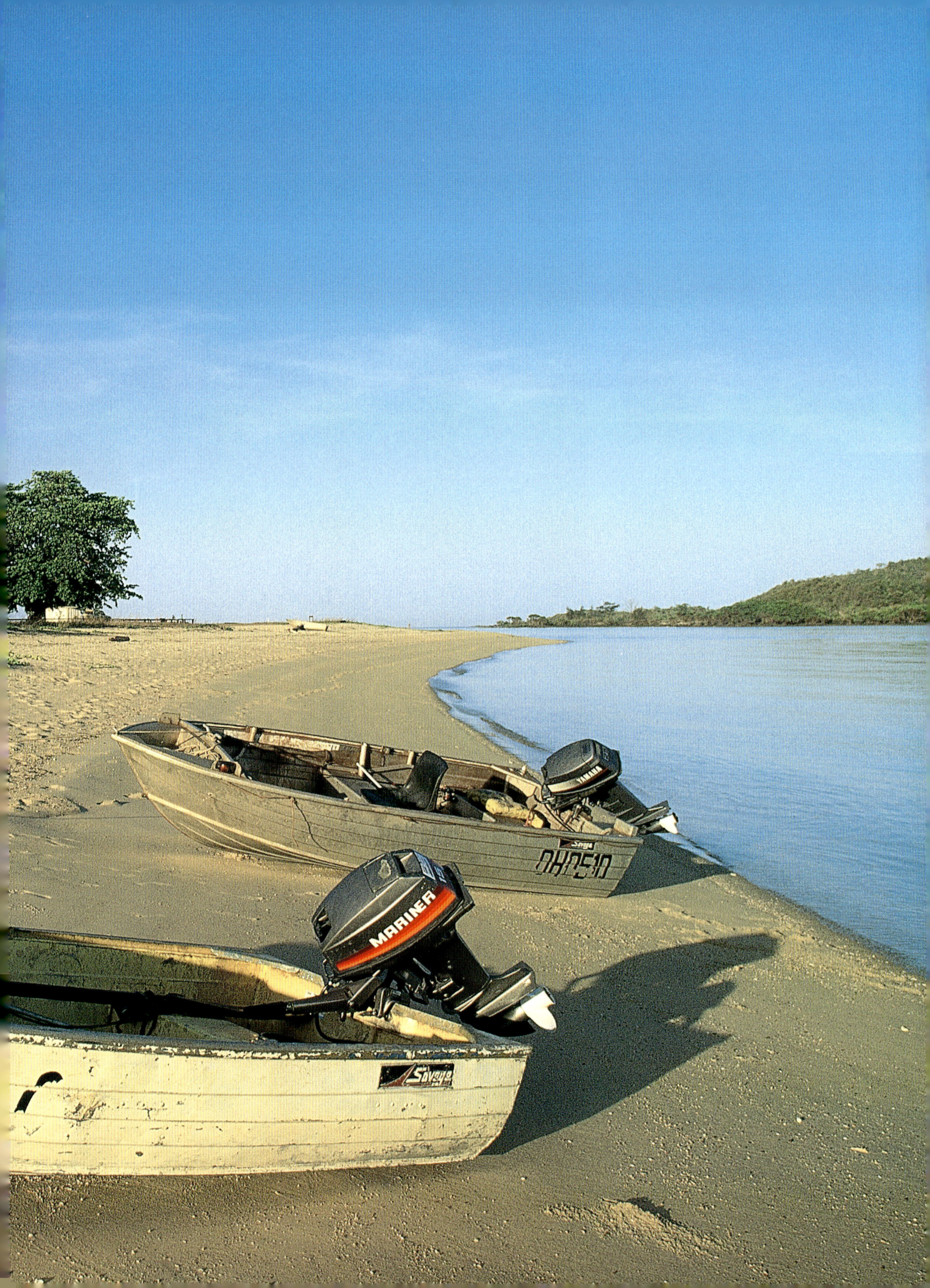
MARINER

THE FAR NORTH - *Lizard Island*

above: Royalty and film stars are among those who know that on Lizard Island, the Reef's most northerly resort, secluded luxury is complemented by some of the best diving in the world.

top: The diver is almost dwarfed by this huge potato cod which weighs more than most human beings. At the famous Cod Hole off Lizard Island, cod are so tame they can be handfed.

right: It may look like something out of Star Trek, but it's actually a delicately fringed soft coral, made up of millions of polyps connected by fleshy tissue, and quite common in Reef waters.

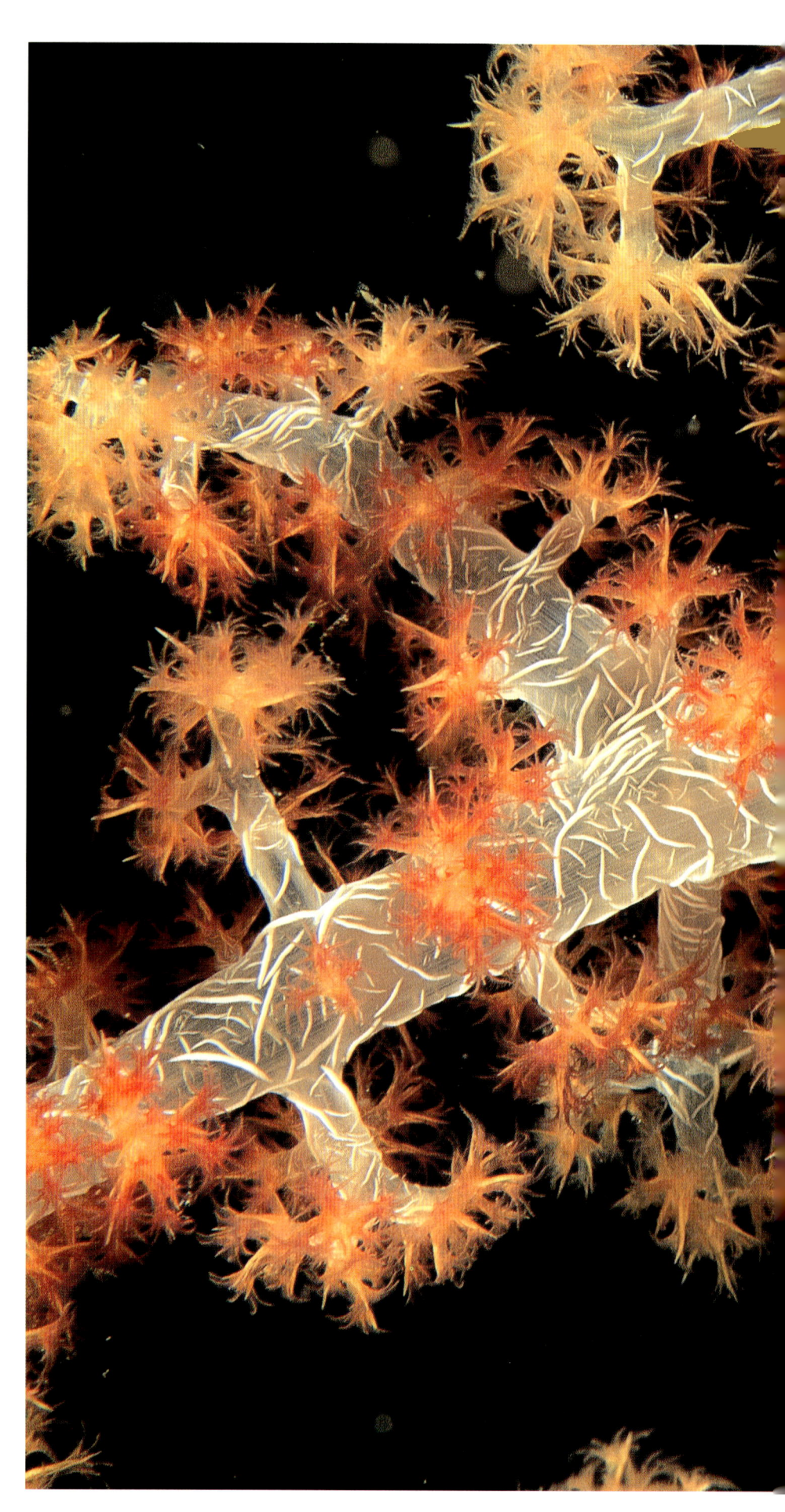

54

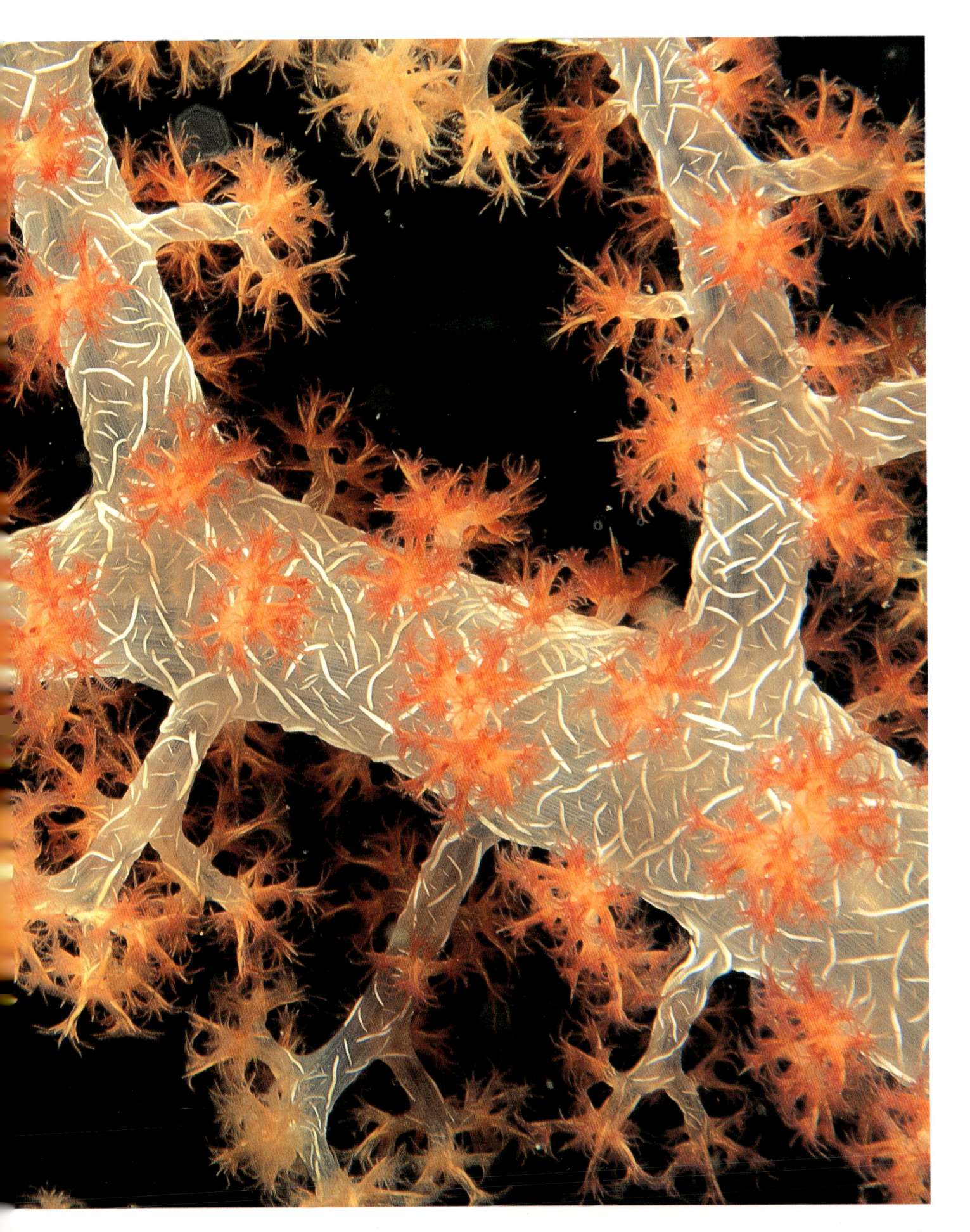

Lizard Island - THE FAR NORTH

THE FAR NORTH - *Cooktown*

Cooktown - THE FAR NORTH

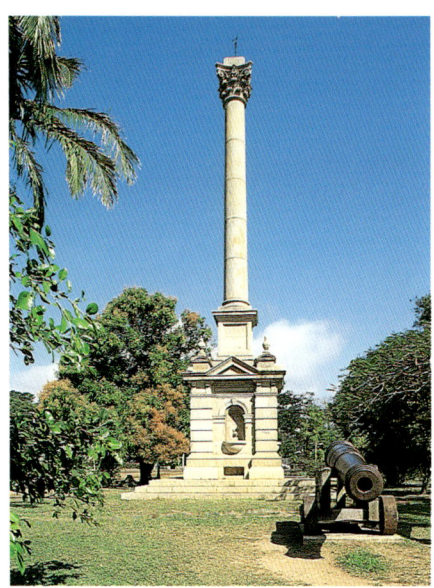

above: Cooktown is the most northerly major settlement on Australia's east coast. The navigator's memorial has pride of place in the town that bears his name.

top: Life moves slowly in northern Queensland. On this old wooden bridge across the Annan River north of Cooktown, there's always time to sit and think.

left: When he sailed up the coast in 1770, Captain Cook would have seen sunsets like this one at Cooktown, with the Endeavour River in the background.

THE FAR NORTH - *Cape Tribulation*

Cape Tribulation - THE FAR NORTH

opposite: In the brooding silence of the deep rainforest at Cape Tribulation, life proceeds at a much slower pace than the energetic frenzy of the coastal resorts.

top: 'Earth has not anything to show more fair'. Reef, beach and rainforest join together to create the majesty of the Cape Tribulation National Park.

above: The delicate ecological balance of tropical plants and animals is on display, accessible but undisturbed, at the Rainforest Habitat Park near Port Douglas.

THE FAR NORTH - *Daintree*

above: 'Up the lazy river...': A tourist boat cruises along on the Humbug Reach of the Daintree River in an endless search for lurking crocodiles.

left: Very rare and very shy, the Boyd's Forest Dragon inhabits the deepest parts of the Daintree rainforest, where it can occasionally be spotted by night walkers.

opposite: On the banks of the Daintree River during the wet season, clouds gather their strength before they thunder down in a dramatic tropical storm.

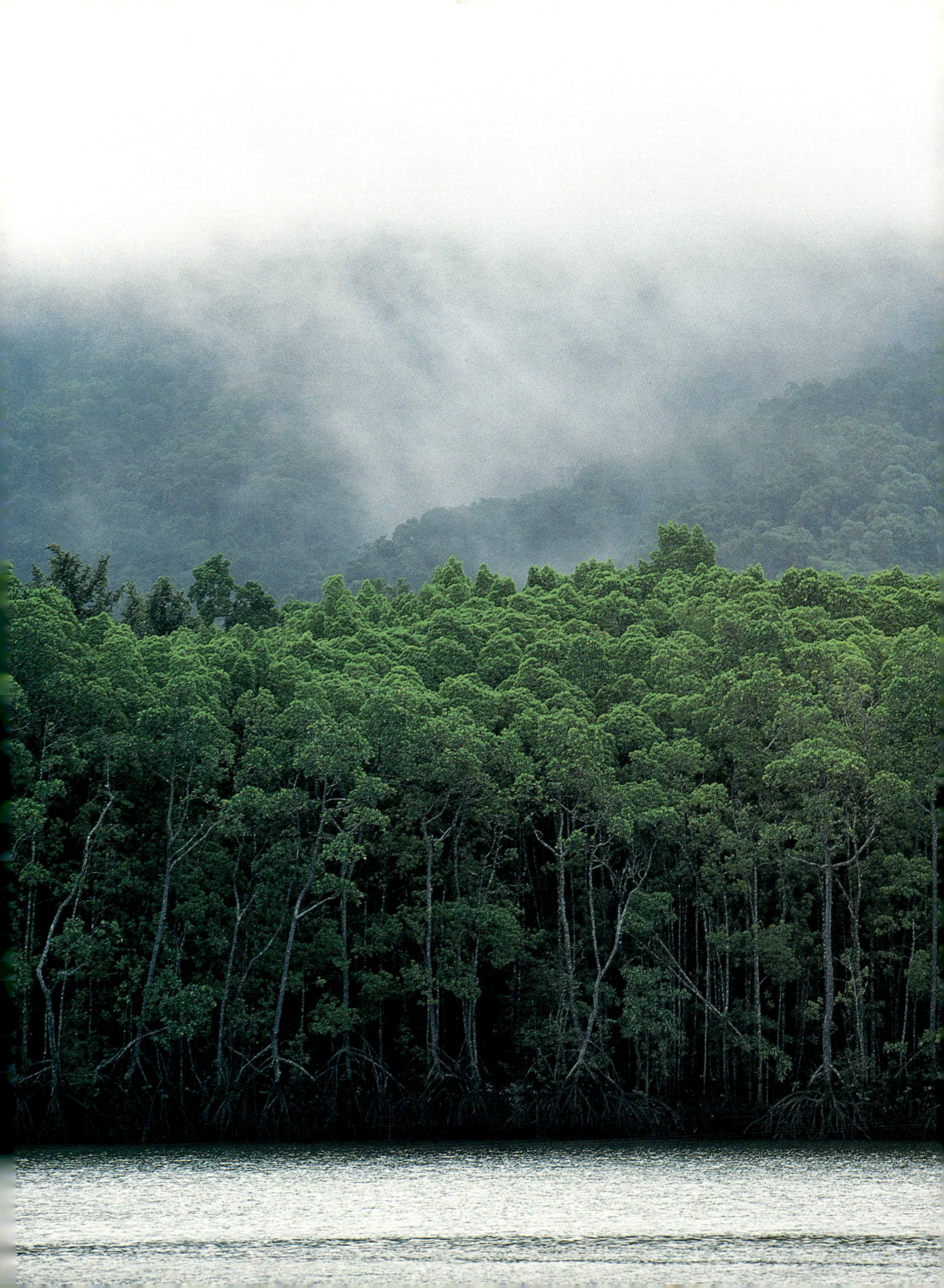

THE FAR NORTH - *Mossman Gorge*

below: The clear waters of Mossman Gorge offer endless opportunities for swimming, canoeing, or just paddling about.

Port Douglas - THE FAR NORTH

above: Beautiful beaches like this one between Cairns and Port Douglas tempt drivers passing through to stop the car and take a break for half an hour, or an hour, or even longer.

top: The sleepy fishing village of Port Douglas is now one of the north coast's most fashionable resort towns, an excellent base for deep sea fishing and expeditions to the outer Reef.

following pages: Shopping, fishing, swimming, boating or simply sitting and sipping coffee while watching the world go by. Port Douglas offers everything the heart could desire — at a price.

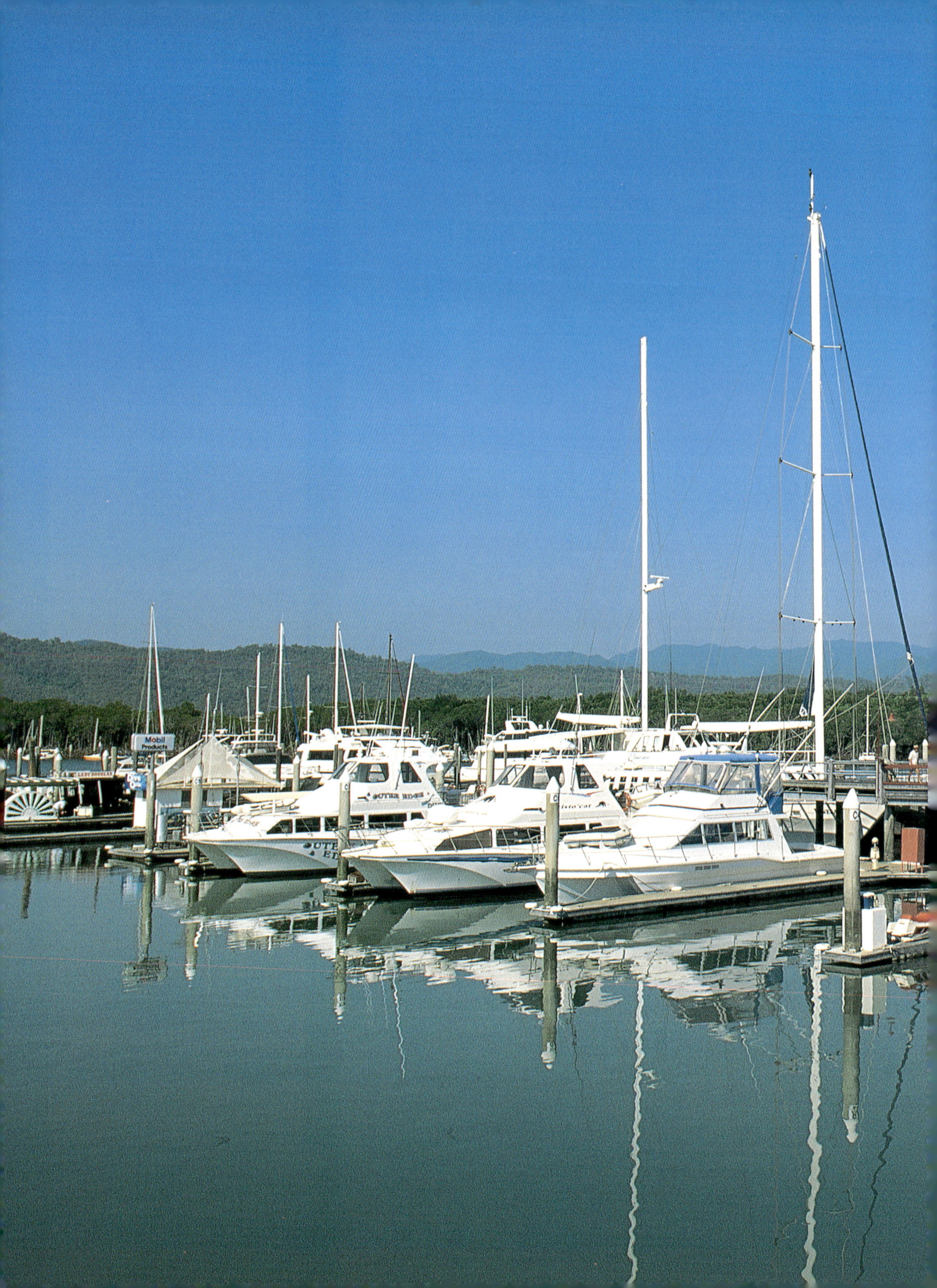
Mobil
Products

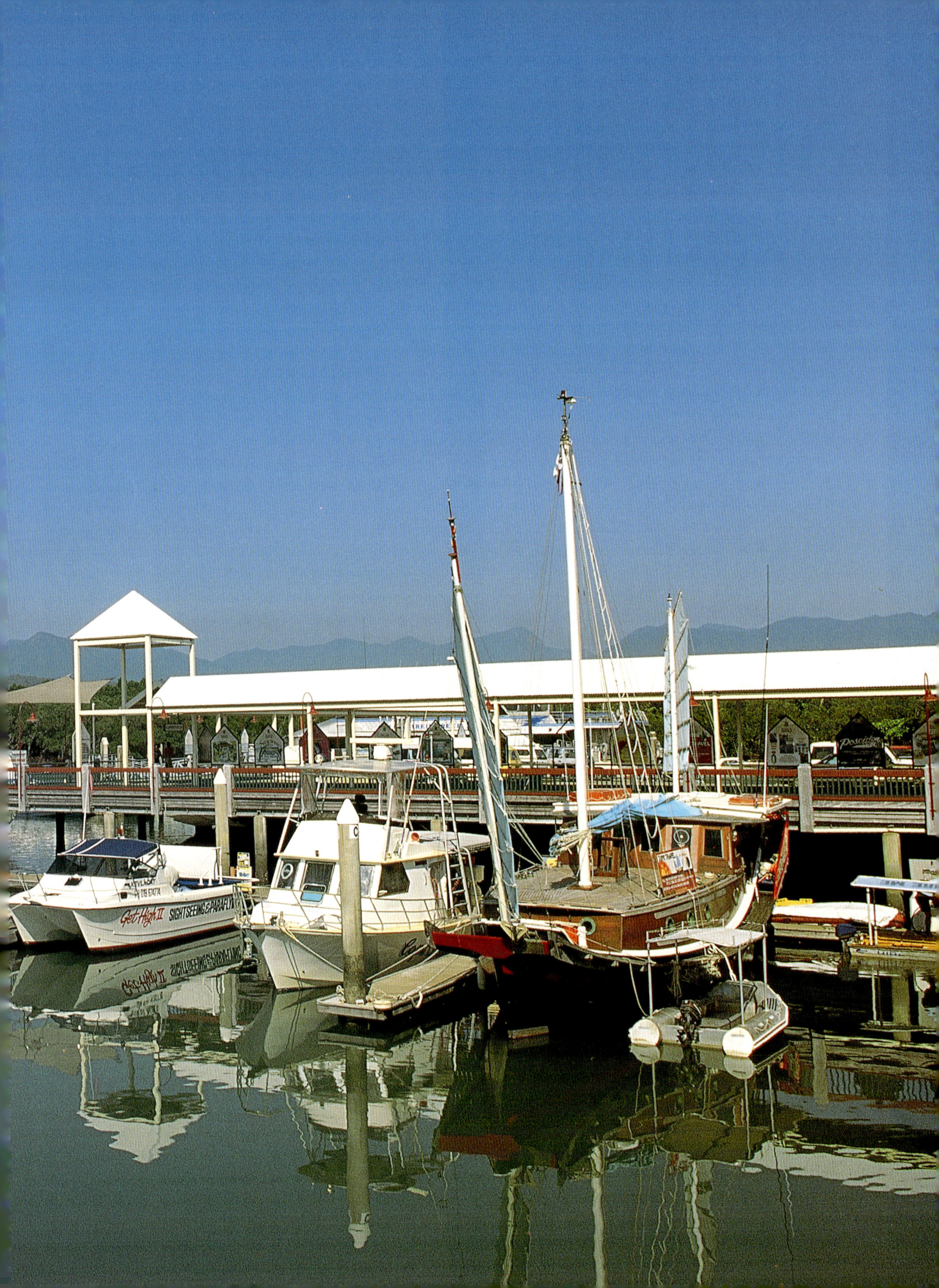
Get High II

THE FAR NORTH - *Michaelmas Cay*

above: Far away from islands where daytrippers congregate, swimmers at Michaelmas Cay relax in the calm clear waters, knowing that only the noisy seabirds can interrupt their peace.

left: Because there are so few predators, many islands and cays have developed into breeding grounds for tropical birds. A brown booby with her chicks gazes fearlessly at the camera.

Palm Cove - THE FAR NORTH

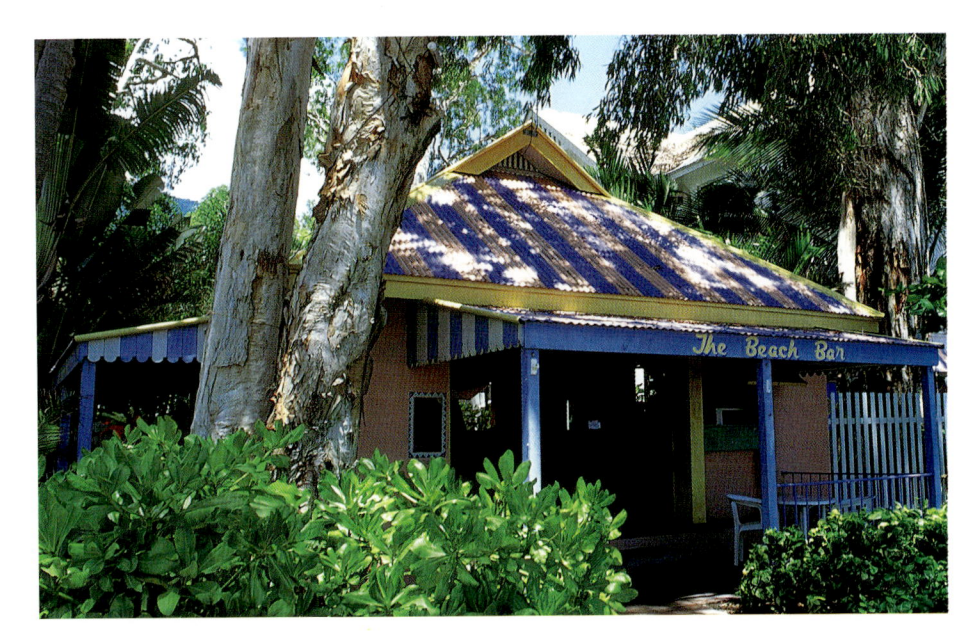

left: Even the architecture is colourful in the tropics. This cheerful little shop at Palm Cove nestles beneath the branches of the huge eucalypts that are common on this part of the coast.

below: It's possible to find solitude even at Palm Cove which, with its sheltered beaches and easy access to Cairns, is one of the most popular resorts in far north Queensland.

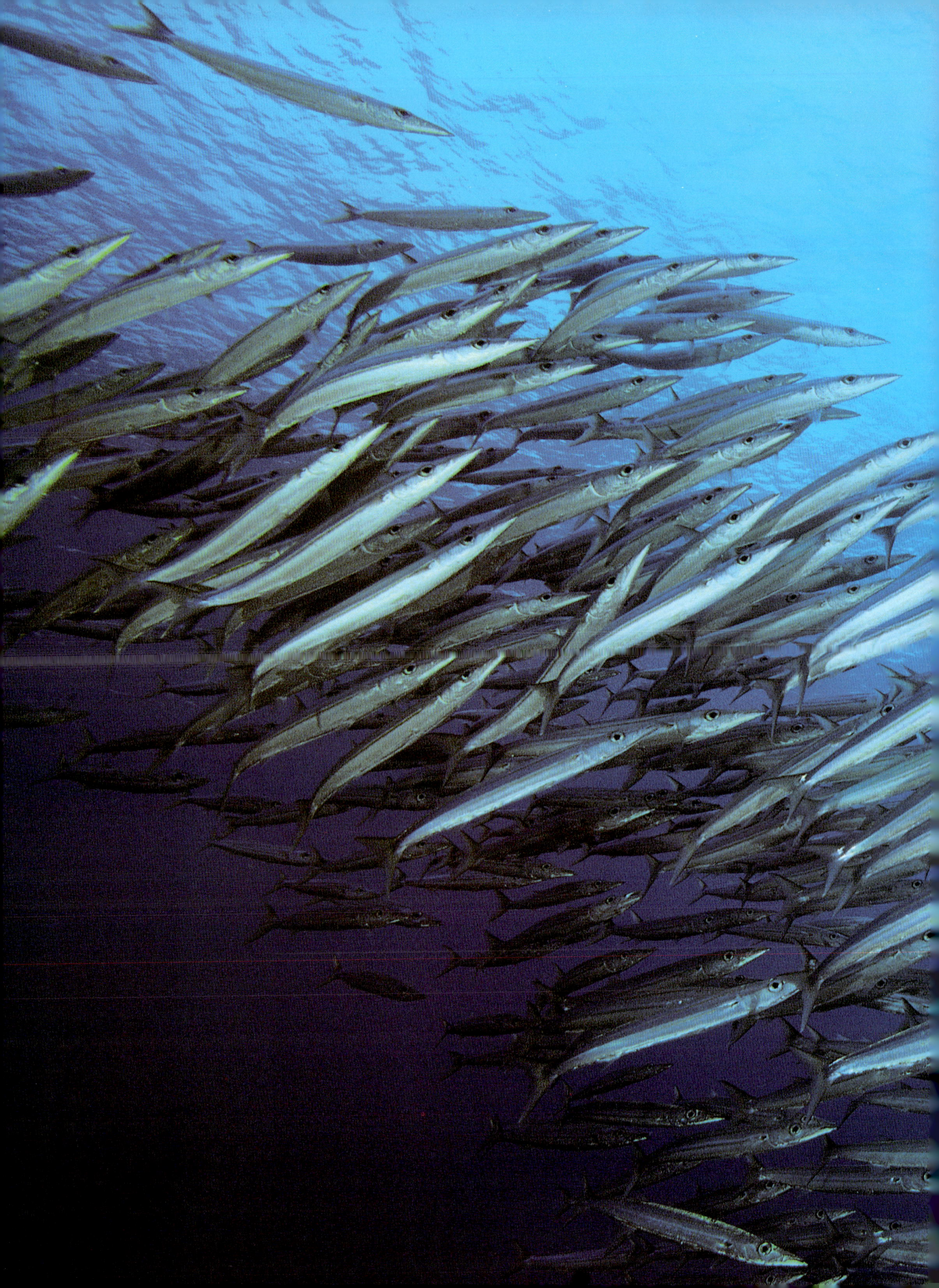

CAIRNS
Queensland's northern playground

*F*ounded in 1876 as a port for the inland goldfields, the sleepy little seaside town of Cairns is now developing into an increasingly sophisticated tourist city of major importance. Five-star hotels are springing up along the waterfront, and 1996 saw the opening of the striking Reef Hotel Casino and a convention centre of international standards. Cairns is also the home of the Great Barrier Reef Dive Festival, where diving experts from all over the world meet every year for a series of events combining eco-tourism, education and adventure.

Cairns nevertheless retains its endearing country town atmosphere — it is small and compact, with much of the colonial architecture of the 19th century still intact. There is a strong Aboriginal presence — indigenous culture can be experienced either through the traditional artefacts at the many galleries and shops or on cultural tours where local people demonstrate the delights of bush tucker and the curiosities of bush medicine.

The town is an ideal base for a north Queensland holiday — it has exquisite beaches both north and south, and is the best place to book trips to the outlying islands as well as to the World Heritage rainforests of the region. It is also the starting point for one of the north's most popular tourist attractions — the scenic train ride through the Barron Gorge to the hinterland rainforest village of Kuranda, with its picturesque railway station.

Cairns is only a stone's throw from the Barrier Reef — busy little Green Island is a 45-minute boat ride away, with trips further afield to uninhabited cays available for serious divers, while a short trip in a light plane gives access to some of the most popular (or exclusive) resort islands like Dunk, Bedarra and Orpheus. But even with all these attractions it is still possible to find a lonely stretch of beach to walk on or a patch of rainforest with nobody else around, and to feel that you've really got away from it all.

opposite: Sunlight filters through the canopy to the floor of the Atherton Tableland rainforest.
previous pages: A silvery school of slender barracuda darts through sunlit tropical waters.

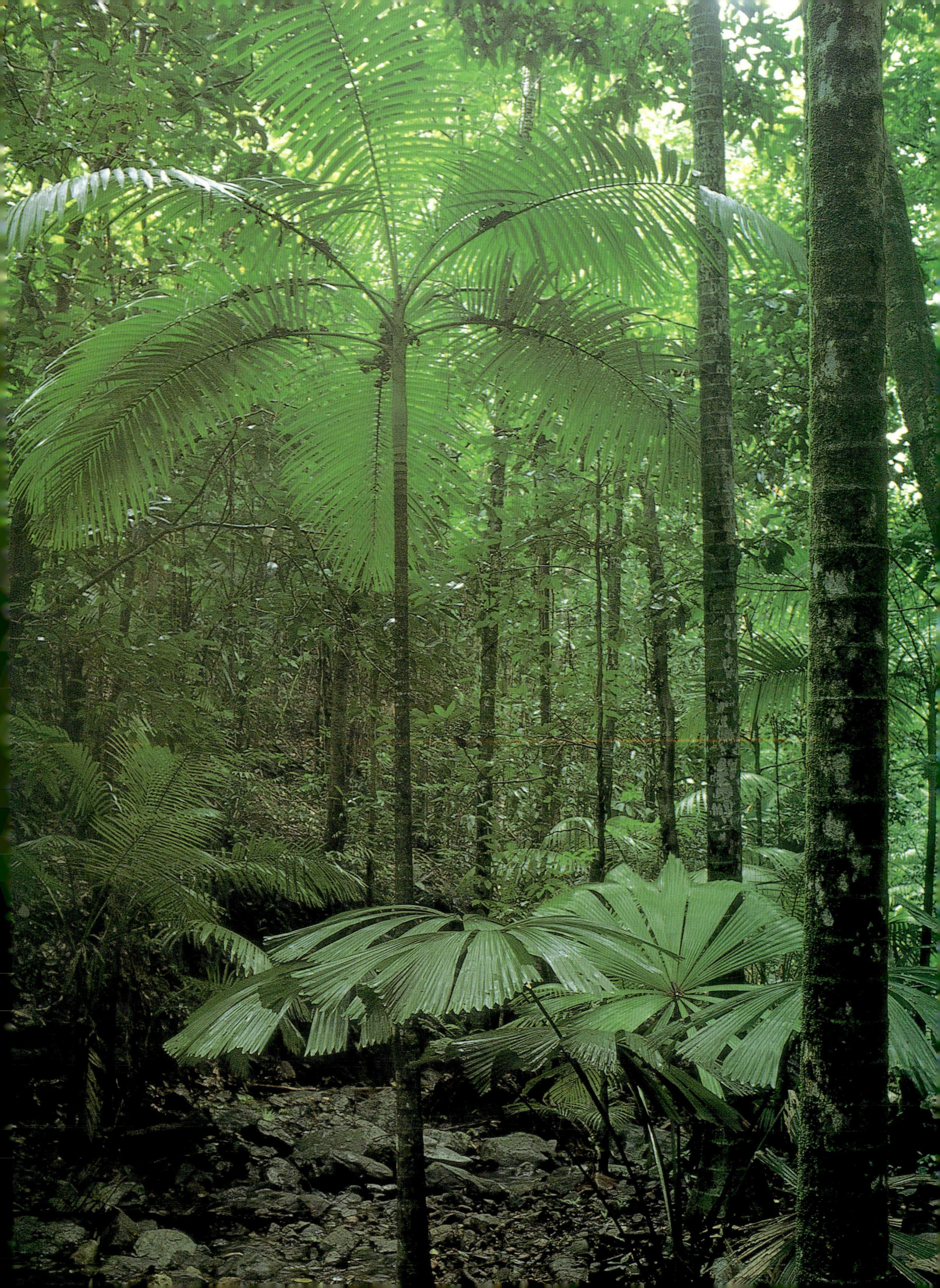

CAIRNS - *Local attractions*

above: For those who find whitewater rafting too tame, there's always bungee jumping, a sport growing in popularity in Cairns.

top: Exotic orchids flourish in the tropical garden inside the dome of the Reef Hotel and Casino in Cairns.

top right: As the sun goes down, Cairns lights up. Tropical palms are dwarfed by the bulk of the city's Boland Centre.

bottom right: Cairns is not only a popular tourist centre, but a busy port catering for everything from cargo ships to ocean cruisers.

Local attractions - CAIRNS

CAIRNS - *Green Island and the outer reef*

Green Island and the outer reef - CAIRNS

opposite: Yachts, motor boats, catamarans and even seaplanes make regular daytrips from Cairns to unspoilt coral cays and sandy reefs like this.

top: Green Island, not far from Cairns, is a popular tourist destination, but the best snorkelling is off its outer reefs, rather than close inshore.

above: Every day, hundreds of people come to Green Island in cruise ships to shop, laze in the sun and visit the Melanesian display centre.

CAIRNS - *Kuranda*

above: The view from the Skyrail, which takes passengers from coastal Cairns to Kuranda on the Atherton Tableland, takes in rainforest, agricultural land and ocean.

top: Tips on throwing a boomerang or playing a didgeridoo, and a different view of Australian history can be found at the Tjapukai Aboriginal Cultural Park, a tourist complex dedicated to preserving and explaining traditional Aboriginal culture.

right: This little steam train has been chugging up the mountain for many years, leaving a quaint old station outside Cairns for a picturesque one-hour journey through the Barron Gorge to Kuranda and the rainforests of the Atherton Tableland.

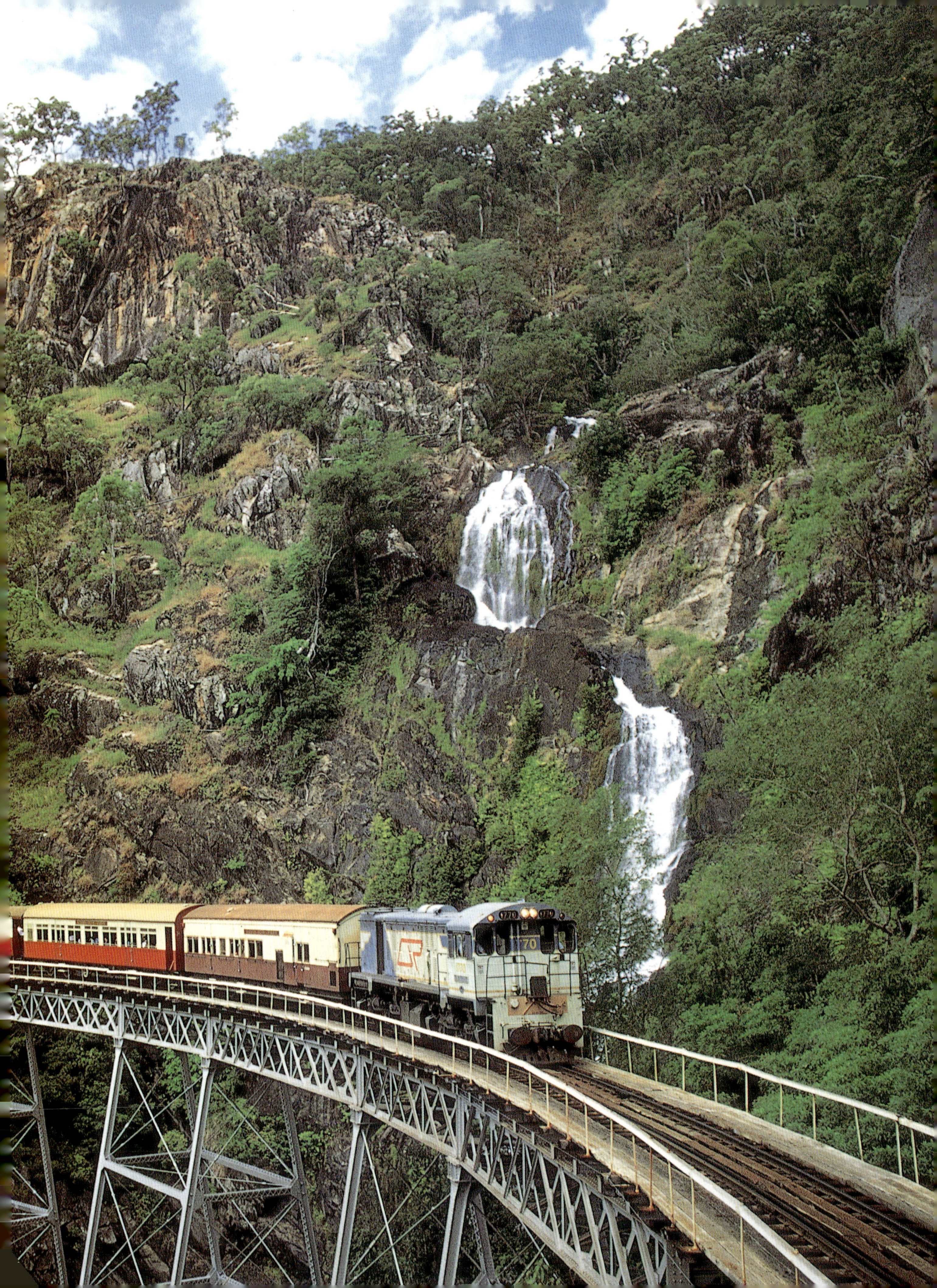

CAIRNS - *Kuranda*

above: Even during the dry season, waterfalls cascade down from the Atherton Tableland to the coast.

Atherton Tableland - CAIRNS

left: The town of Chillagoe, 150 kilometres inland from Cairns, boasts some stunning limestone caves. This one is part of the Fairy Grotto in the Chillagoe National Park.

below: Tropical sunsets are always spectacular, especially when storm clouds are gathering. The sugar-growing centre of Mareeba, near Cairns, awaits an evening downpour.

following pages: Filtered light, murmuring insects, and rich dank undergrowth — deep in the tropical rainforest the world is filled with many shades of green.

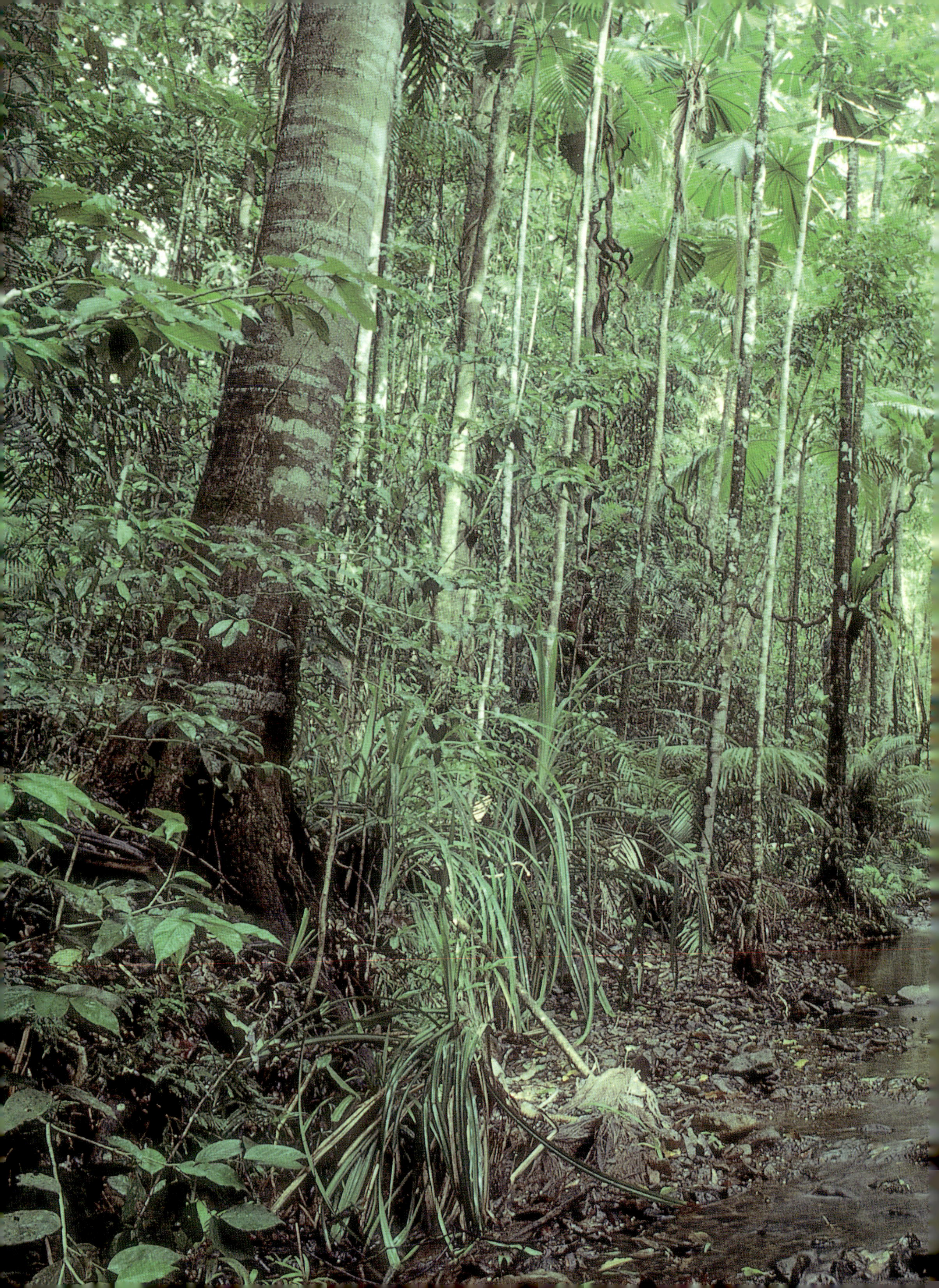

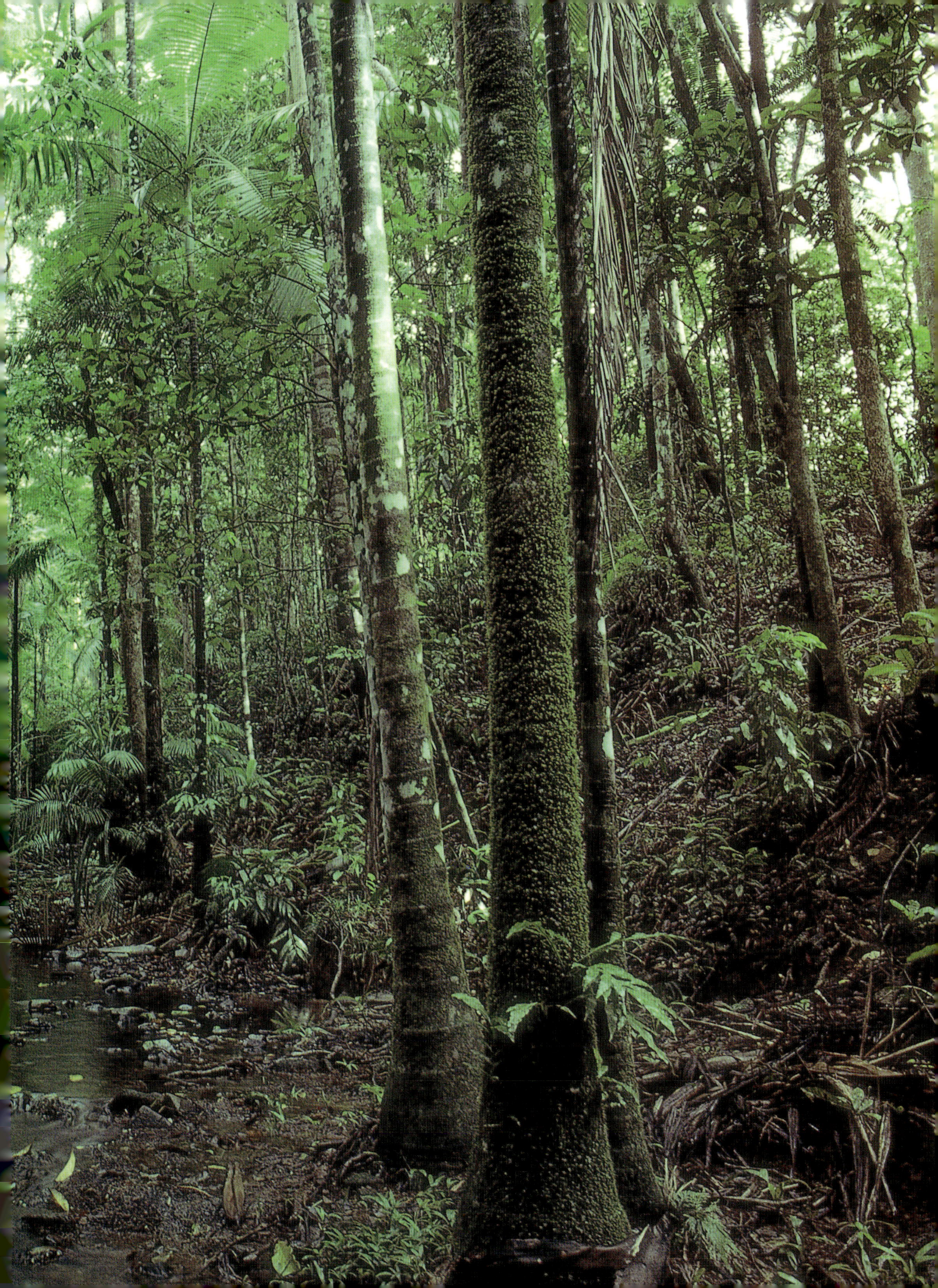

CAIRNS - *Atherton Tableland*

above: Enter the Royal Arch Caves through the Archways, part of the massive limestone cave system in the Chillagoe National Park.

top: A self-absorbed duck paddles lazily on Lake Barrine, a crater lake on the Atherton Tableland surrounded by huge kauri pines.

right: Millaa Millaa, inland from Cairns, forms part of the popular Waterfall Circuit which also takes in the beautiful Zillie and Elinjaa falls.

Atherton Tableland - CAIRNS

CAIRNS – *Innisfail*

Innisfail - CAIRNS

above: The tea plant, which was introduced relatively recently into Australia, thrives in the climate of the wet tropics. This makes Innisfail, one of Australia's wettest towns, an ideal spot for tea plantations.

top: Innisfail's claims to fame include superb boating facilities on the Johnstone River, tea and sugar plantations, and an annual rainfall of 3.641 metres.

left: A mighty gum is silhouetted against the raging flames of the annual sugarcane burn-off. Australia is one of the world's major producers of sugar, most of it grown in north Queensland.

CAIRNS - *Tully and Mission Beach*

Tully and Mission Beach - CAIRNS

opposite: The river at Tully, about 25 kilometres inland from Cairns, is a popular venue for whitewater rafting. Rafting safaris in the Tully River Gorge are conducted by experienced operators, while landlubbers can watch from vantage points on the banks.

left: The cassowary, like the emu, is a large flightless bird. Although its distinctive helmet and blue and red colouring make it the darling of photographers, it is a vicious bird which has been known to kill human beings with its knife-like claw.

below: The white sandy beaches, banana plantations and sugar cane fields of the Mission Beach area stretch north along the coast towards Cairns. The area is named for the Aboriginal mission which was set up at South Mission Beach in 1912.

CAIRNS - *Dunk Island*

Dunk Island - CAIRNS

opposite bottom: The spectacular nudibranch is basically a shell-less snail. With its infinite colours and patterns, it is the Reef's most enchanting form of marine life.

opposite top: Another quiet day at Muggy Muggy Beach on Dunk Island. Planted by early European settlers, the coconut palms are not indigenous to Australia.

above: Three shades of blue — sky, sea and swimming pool — are offset by the deep green of giant coconut palms at the Dunk Island resort.

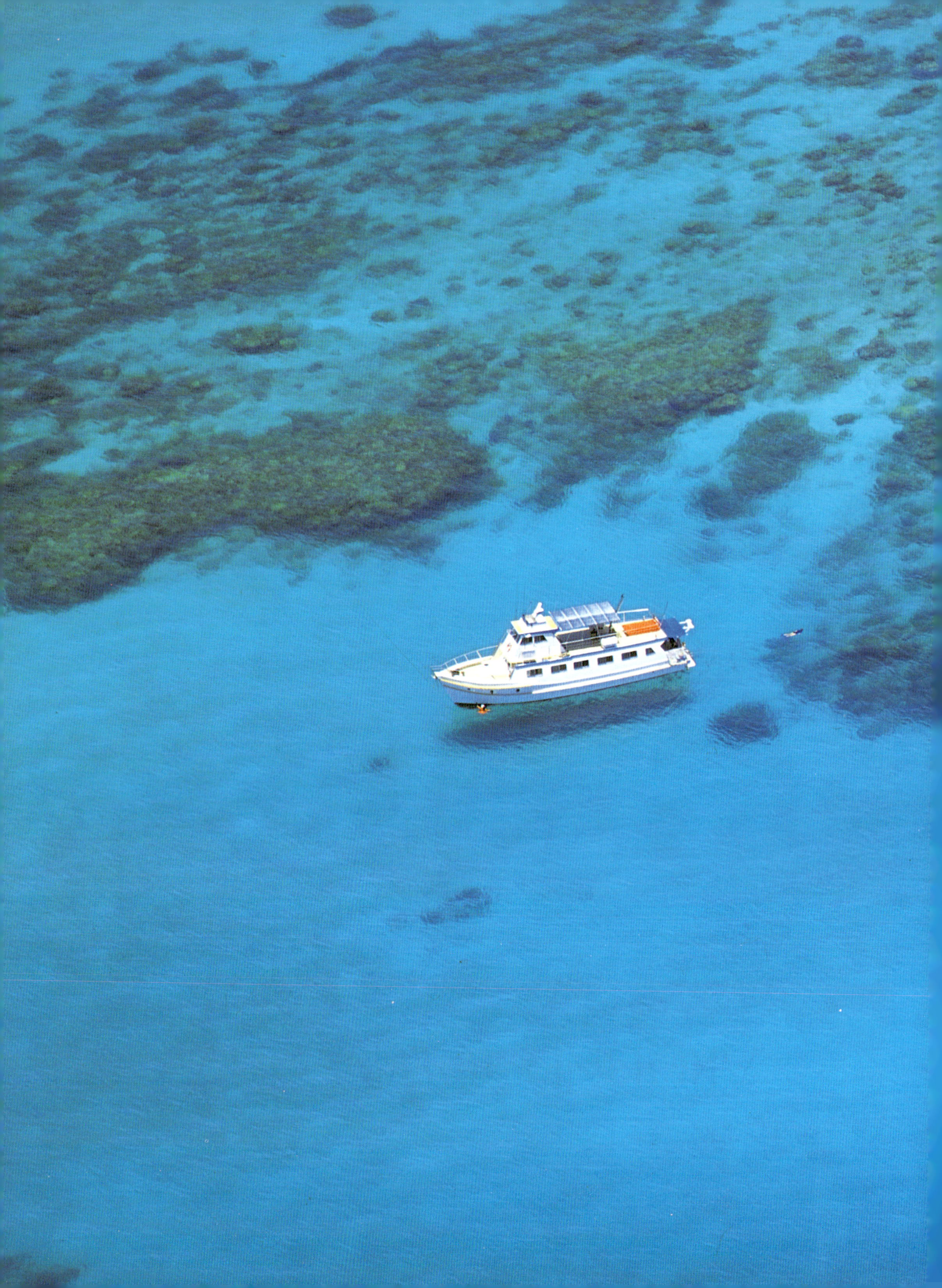

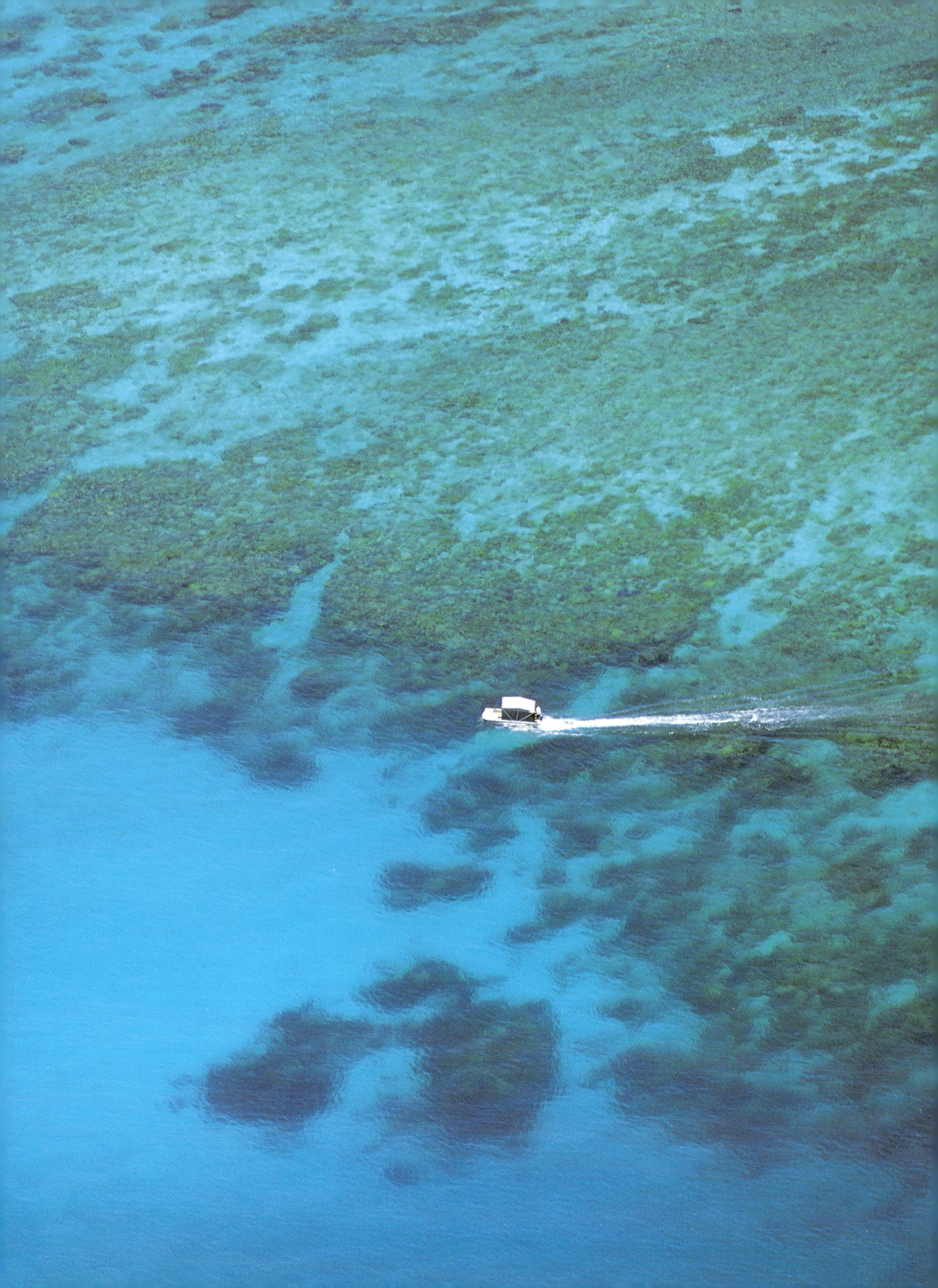

CAIRNS - *Dunk Island*

above: Using their boat as a base, swimmers luxuriate in the warm tropical waters off Dunk Island before retiring to the deck for a cooling drink.

left: The vivid blue of the Ulysses butterfly, the symbol of Dunk Island, makes it the most distinctive of all the insect species on the Reef.

previous pages: Offshore from Dunk Island is a large coral reef, accessible only by boat, which seems a world away from the busy life of the resort.

Bedarra Island - CAIRNS

left: A seaplane cruises in majestic solitude over the Whitsunday Islands, seemingly oblivious to the people far below who are snorkelling, swimming, fishing and making the most of the flawless weather.

below: Bedarra is a luxury island par excellence. Its exclusive resort takes only 36 visitors at a time, most of whom spend their time lazing on the pure white sand of the many secluded coves.

93

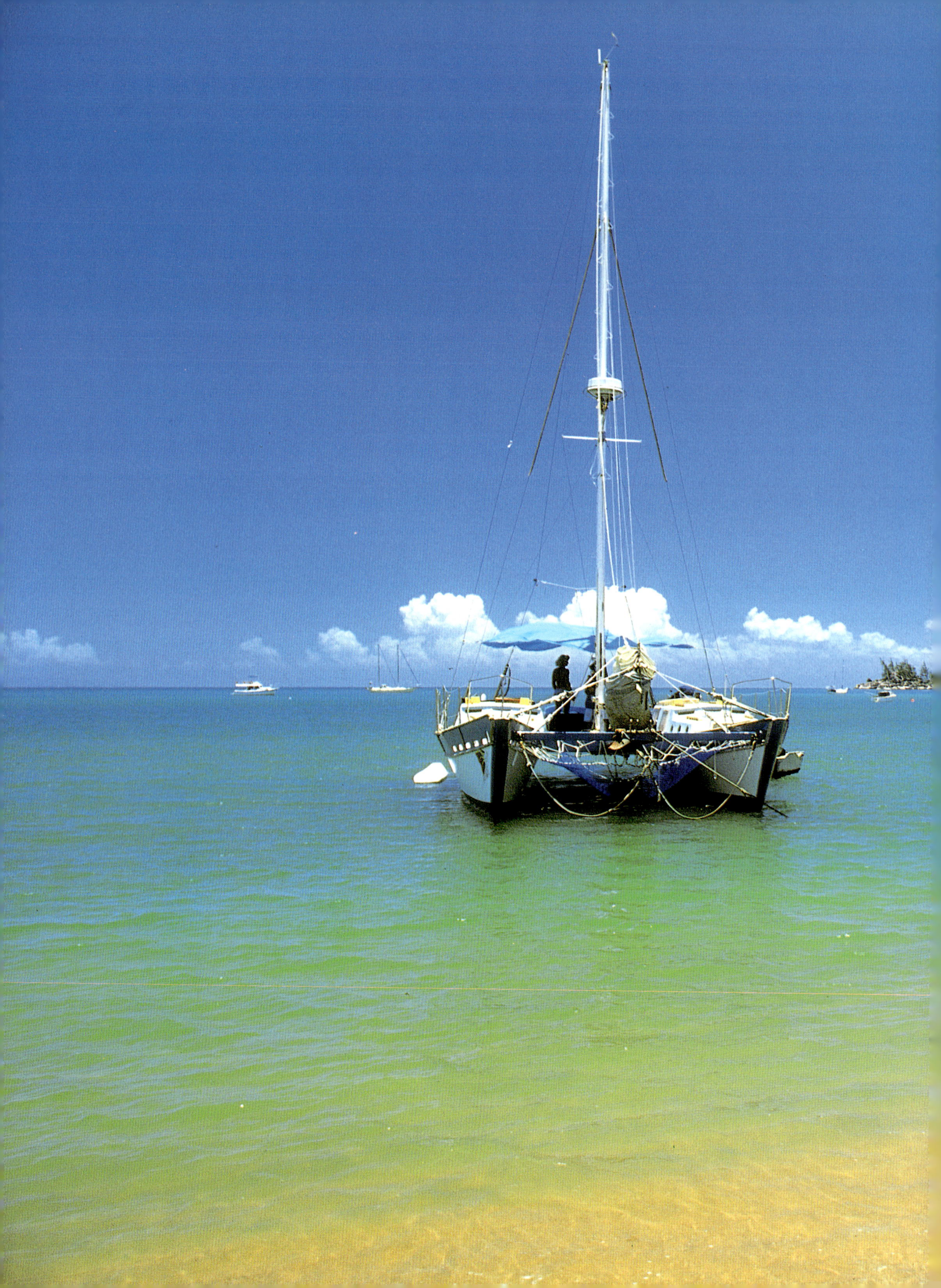

AROUND TOWNSVILLE
Crystal clear waters and a magnetic lifestyle

𝒯ownsville is Australia's largest tropical city. It is also the place to learn all about the Reef without getting your feet wet: in the superb Great Barrier Reef Wonderland you can walk through a perspex tunnel surrounded by sharks, manta rays, potato cod, turtles and other outsize marine creatures. A 3 000 000-litre tank houses a cross-section of a living coral reef, and there are touch pools where it is possible to feel and even pick up some of the smaller marine life forms. Billabong Sanctuary, a few kilometres out of town, is an ideal place to see land-based wildlife like cassowaries, dingoes, kangaroos, crocodiles and kookaburras.

The Sheraton Breakwater Casino provides specialised entertainment for sophisticated thrill seekers, while Townsville's many restaurants (some of them located in the finest buildings of the colonial period) provide a wide variety of cuisines from all over the world.

Regular launches or light aircraft take visitors to Hinchinbrook, Dunk, Bedarra and Orpheus islands, while Magnetic Island, known affectionately by the locals as 'Maggie', is a brief 20 minutes away by fast catamaran. Magnetic Island is ideal for a family holiday, with mid-priced and budget accommodation, hundreds of tiny bays for private swimming, plenty of activities, and a rare chance to see koalas in the wild.

For visitors with a little more time to spare, a trip out west to the old goldmining towns of Charters Towers and Ravenswood gives a glimpse of Queensland's golden past. Some of Australia's most beautiful and characteristic architecture can be found here, with many of the old country pubs with their two-storey bullnose verandas of iron lace restored to their original glory. The region also provides a chance to see some of Queensland's unique bush and scrub country, so different from the lush green of the rainforest.

opposite: This sandy cove at Bowen is typical of the Queensland coastline.
previous pages: A yacht rests at anchor in the crystal waters of Magnetic Island off the Townsville coast.

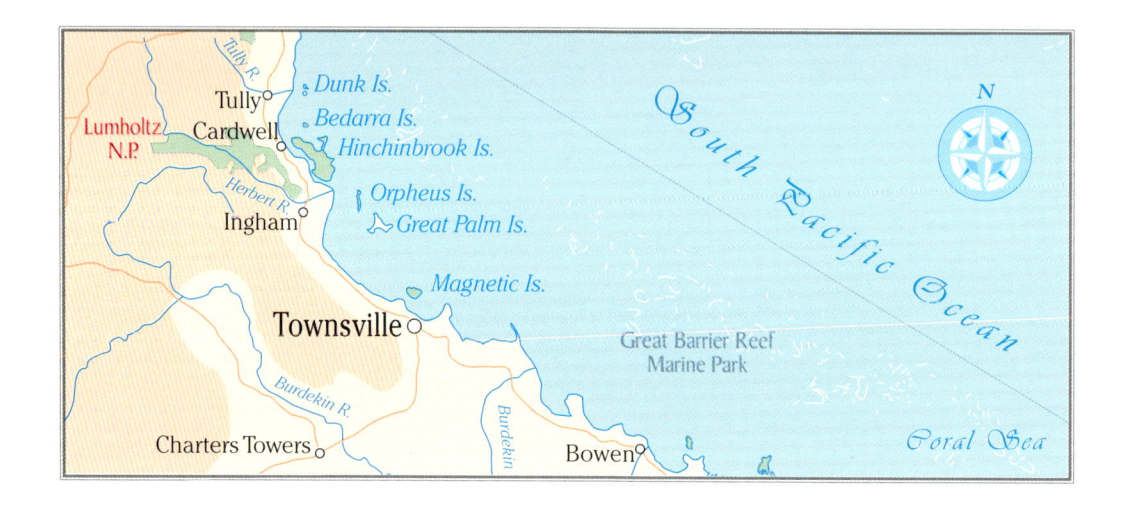

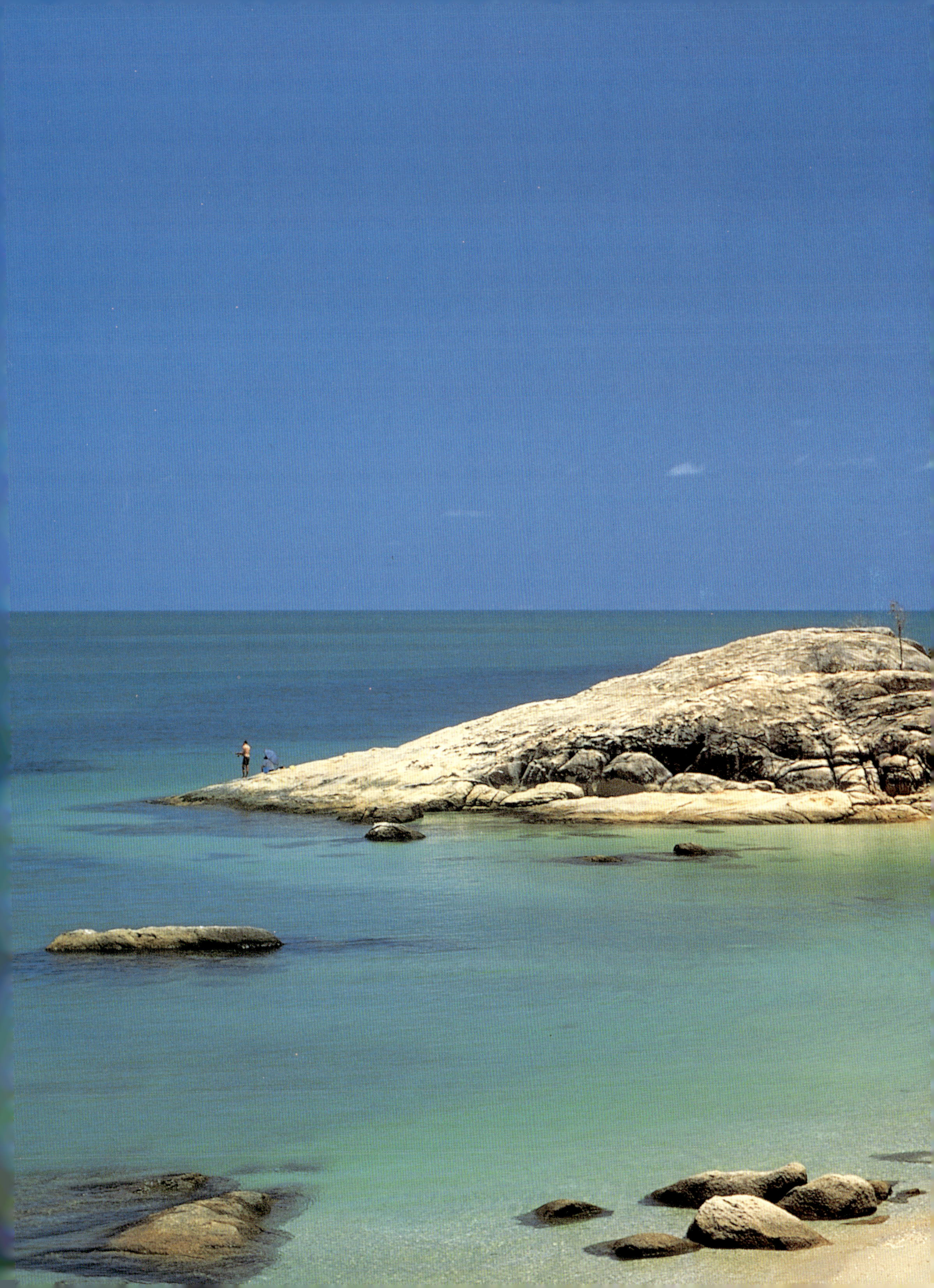

AROUND TOWNSVILLE - *Cardwell*

above: Beach fishing, a popular pastime in northern Queensland, is guaranteed to get results. This woman on the beach at Cardwell will be feasting on trevally, bream, whiting or tailor tonight.

top: The Undara lava tubes, formed 190 000 years ago by a volcano eruption, are well worth the 250-kilometre road or air trip inland. Many visitors stay overnight in converted railway carriages.

Hinchinbrook Island - AROUND TOWNSVILLE

left: The boardwalks at Missionary Bay on Hinchinbrook Island protect the fragile ecological balance of the mangrove swamps and provide ease of access for visitors.

below: Huge mangrove swamps, which provide shelter and nourishment for all kinds of marine creatures, grow in tidal mudflats from seedlings like this one.

bottom: The rugged peaks of Hinchinbrook Island, softened by distance, are reflected in the quiet waters of the Herbert River on the mainland.

following pages: A river winds its way down from the heavily vegetated Hinchinbrook Island range to the sweeping sands at Zoe Bay on the island's east coast.

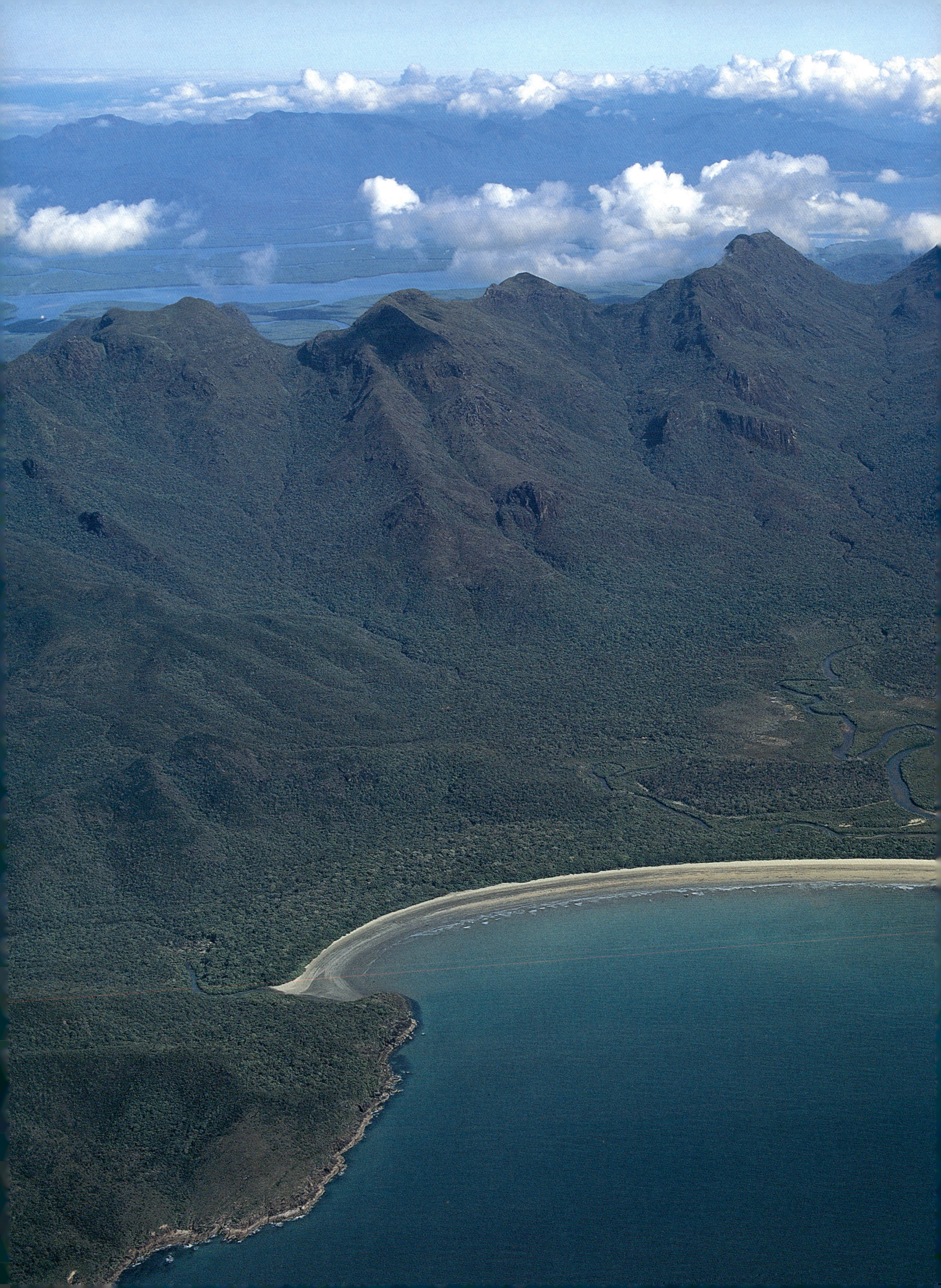

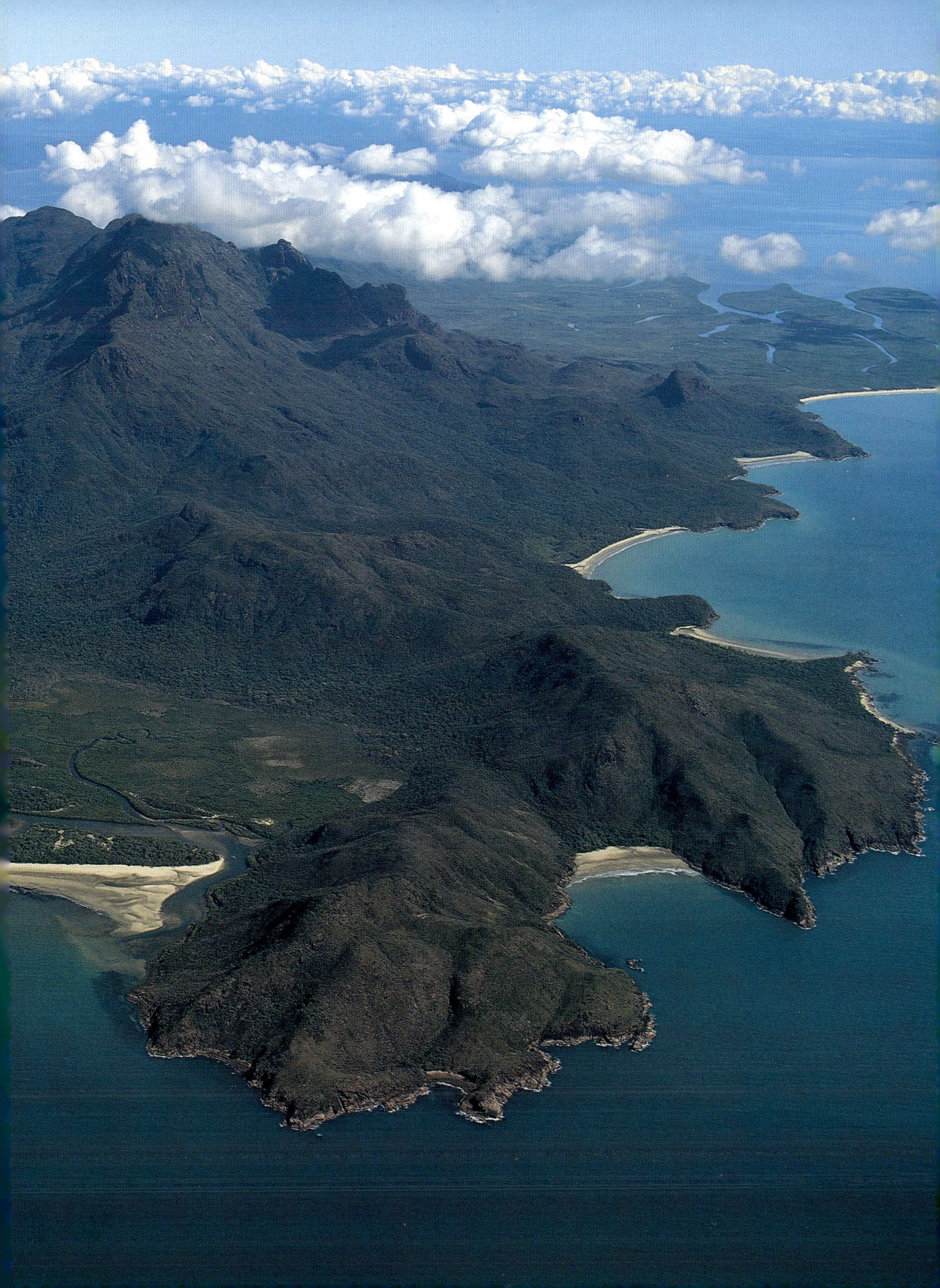

AROUND TOWNSVILLE - *Orpheus Island*

left: Most of the waters around glorious Orpheus Island, one of the Palm Islands group, are zoned Marine National Park B — 'look but don't touch'. Activities like fishing or shell collecting which remove natural resources are not allowed.

below: Dolphins are plentiful along the Queensland coast all year round. They are often seen frolicking in the wake of pleasure boats, like this pair of Common Dolphins who seem to be showing off their sleek lines for the camera.

Ingham - AROUND TOWNSVILLE

above: Wallaman Falls, inland from Cardwell, are Australia's longest sheer-drop falls. There are camping facilities, but the road is not recommended in wet weather.

right: The setting sun bathes one of the many waterways surrounding sleepy Ingham. The town, known as the gateway to the wet tropics, is situated in the middle of important tea and sugar plantations.

following pages: Just off the highway between Townsville and Ingham is Mount Spec National Park, part of the Wet Tropics World Heritage Area, where golden bowerbirds and ringtail possums are often seen. Camping at Big Crystal Creek is popular with locals and visitors alike.

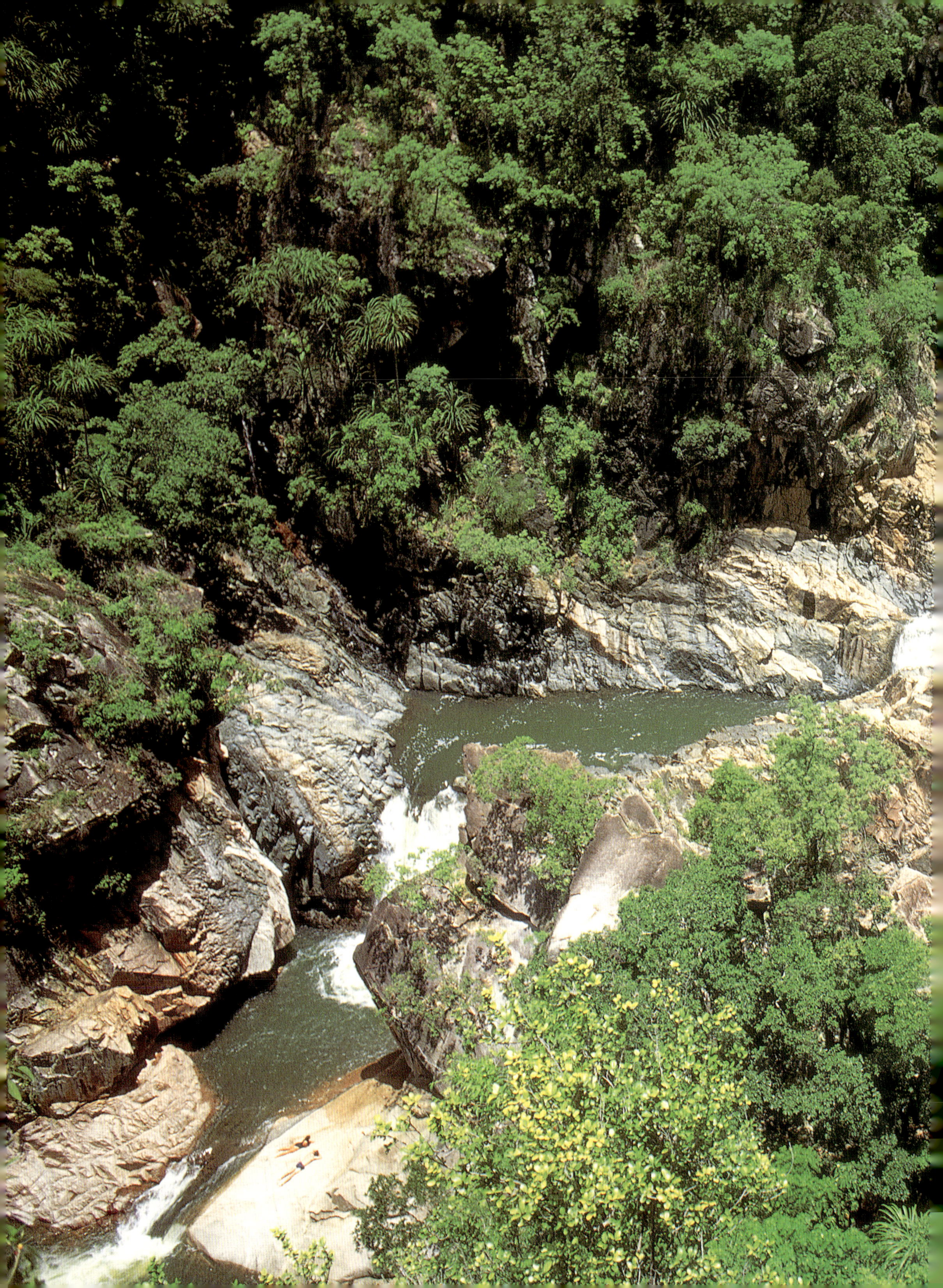

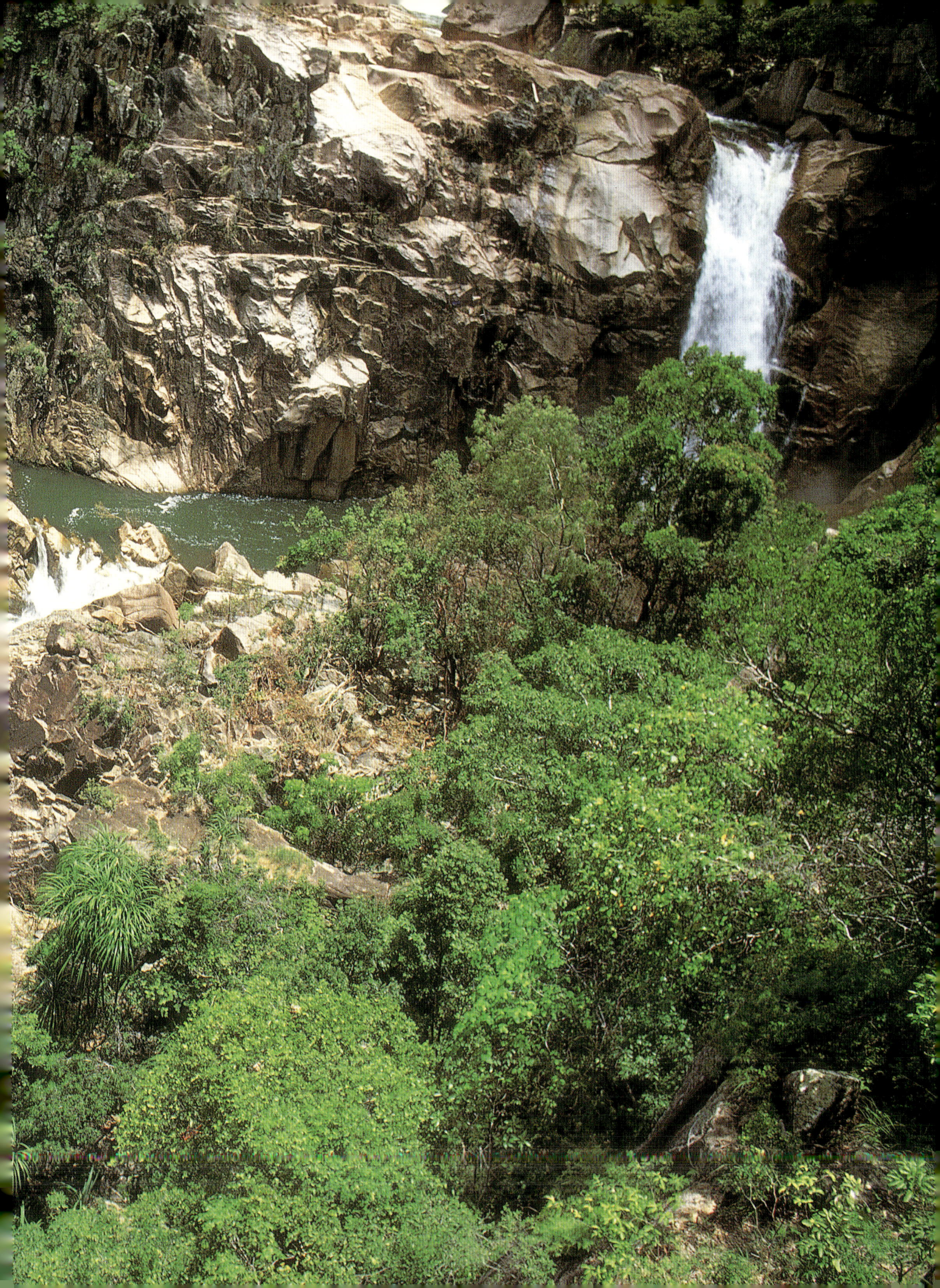

AROUND TOWNSVILLE - *Magnetic Island*

right: It's very cute, but Australia's most popular animal is difficult to spot in the wild. One of the best places to see koalas is on Magnetic Island.

opposite: Magnetic Island offers the delights of those old-fashioned seaside holidays of nostalgic memory — bays, beaches, and paddle boats.

below: The easiest way to get around Magnetic Island is to hire a Mini Moke. These brightly painted little vehicles have names like Troppo and Saucy Susie.

Magnetic Island - AROUND TOWNSVILLE

AROUND TOWNSVILLE - *City sights*

City sights - AROUND TOWNSVILLE

opposite top: Come face to face with sharks, stingrays and colourful reef fish in perfect safety in the 'deep-sea' tunnel at Townsville's Great Barrier Reef.

left: The elegant Customs House in Townsville dates back to the 1860s, when the city was founded as a northern port for agricultural products.

below: Boats at a Townsville marina nestle safely under the watchful gaze of Castle Hill — 285 metres high and affectionately known as a 'near mountain'.

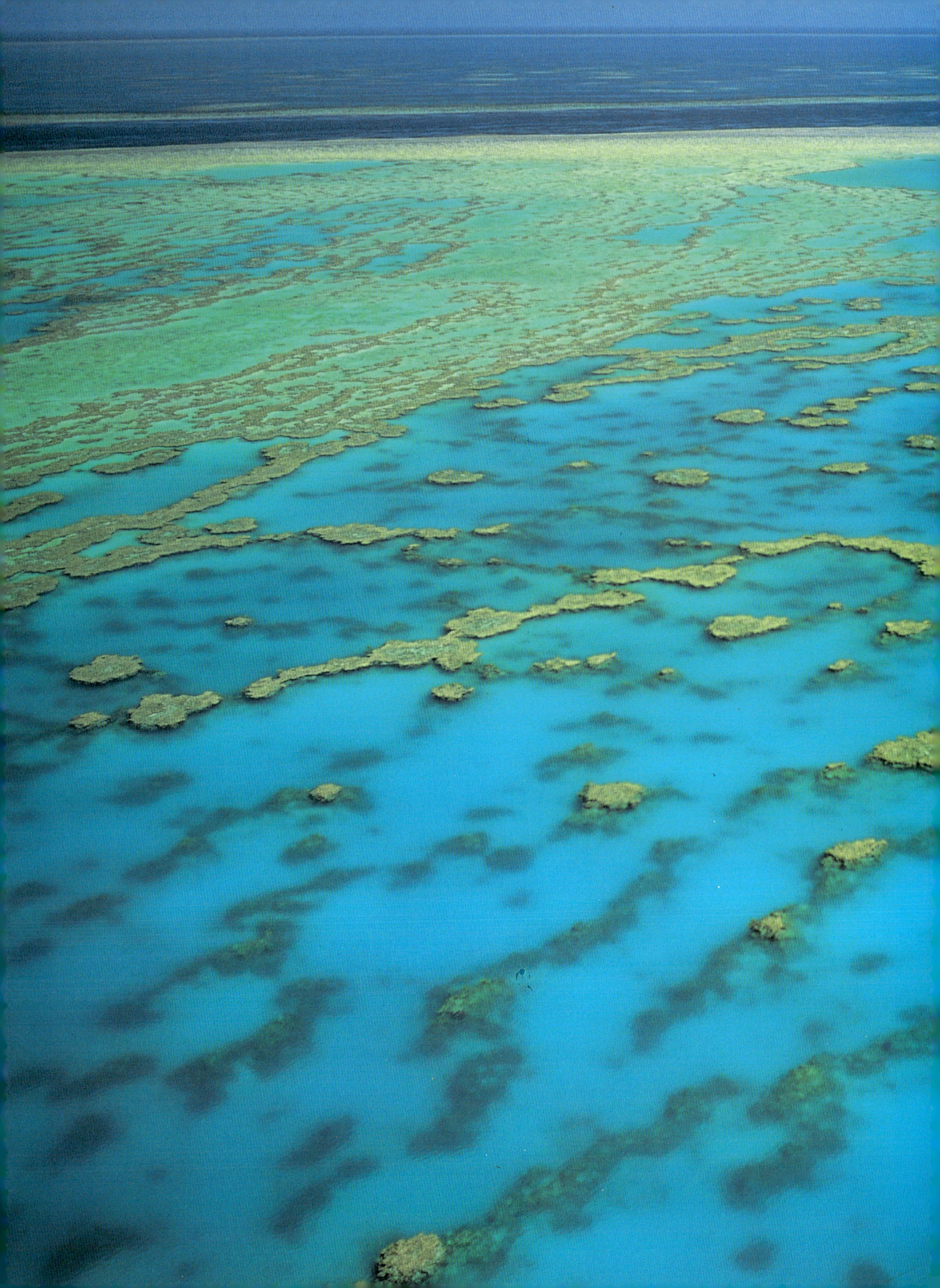

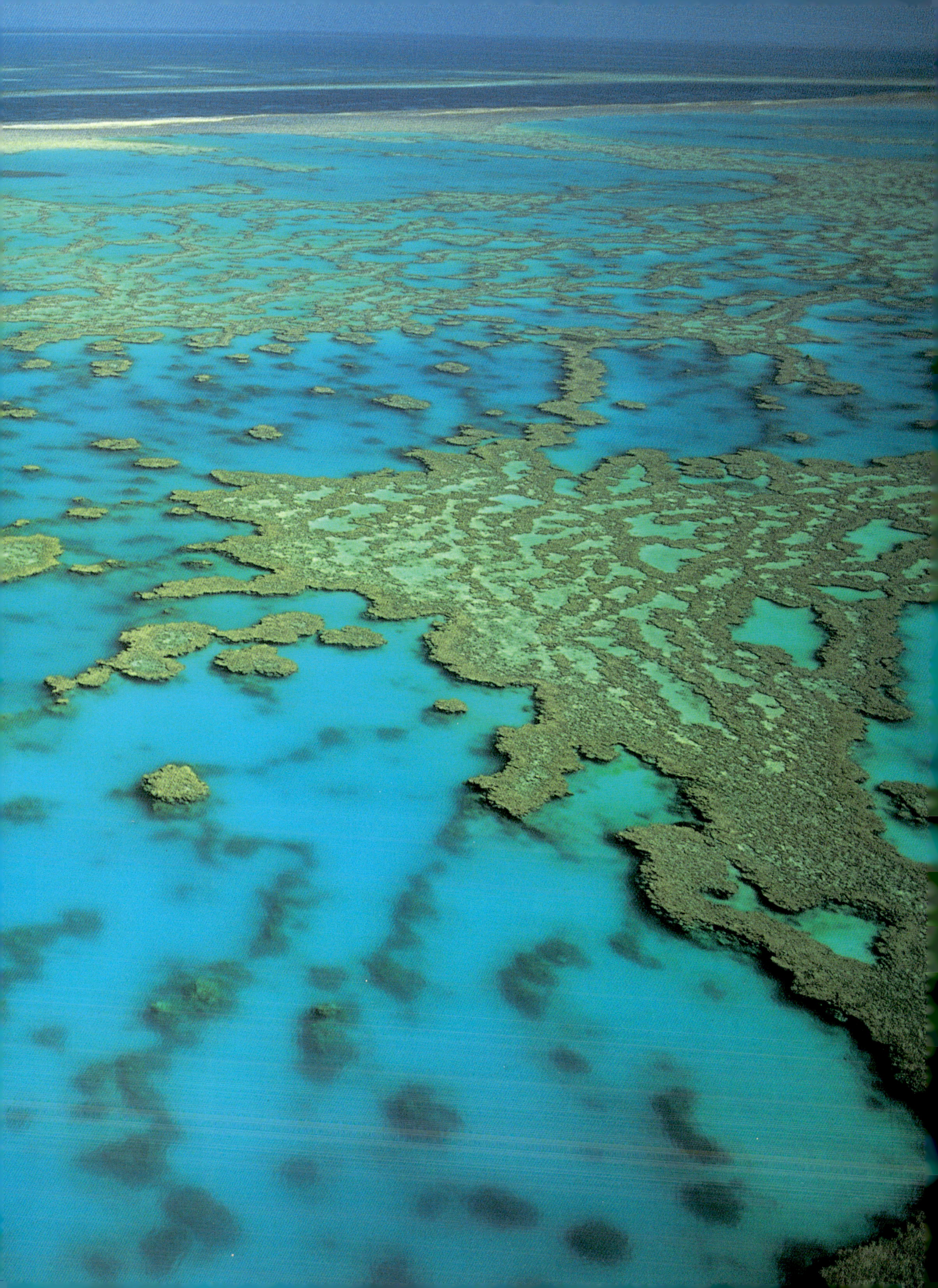

AROUND TOWNSVILLE – *Bowen*

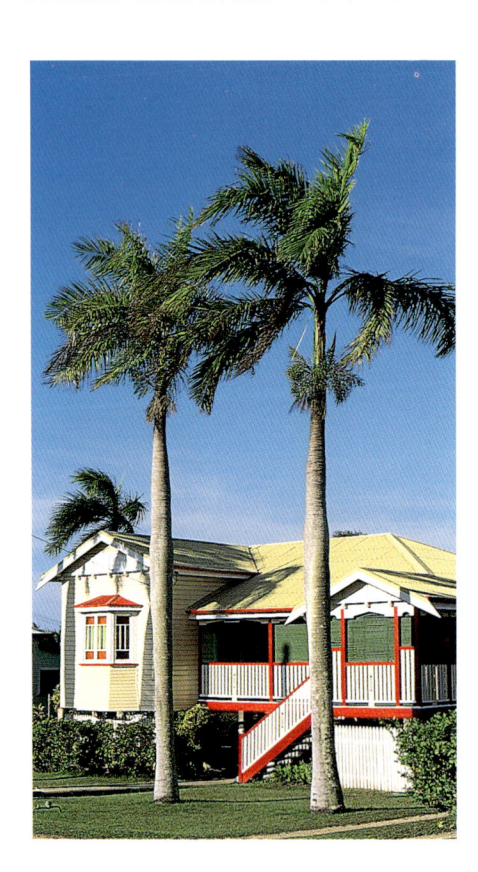

above: Tropical Queensland's climate has generated a distinctive style of architecture. Houses on high stilts create a space for clothes to dry, children to play, and cool breezes to blow through in the wet season.

right: In a universe that seems infinite, small boats are dwarfed by the immensity of sea and sky, and even the mountains of the Bowen coast shrink into insignificance in the glory of the setting sun.

previous pages: From the air, the full extent of the coral formations making up the Great Barrier Reef is easily appreciated. The warm clear waters off Townsville are ideal for the development of reef-building corals.

Bowen - AROUND TOWNSVILLE

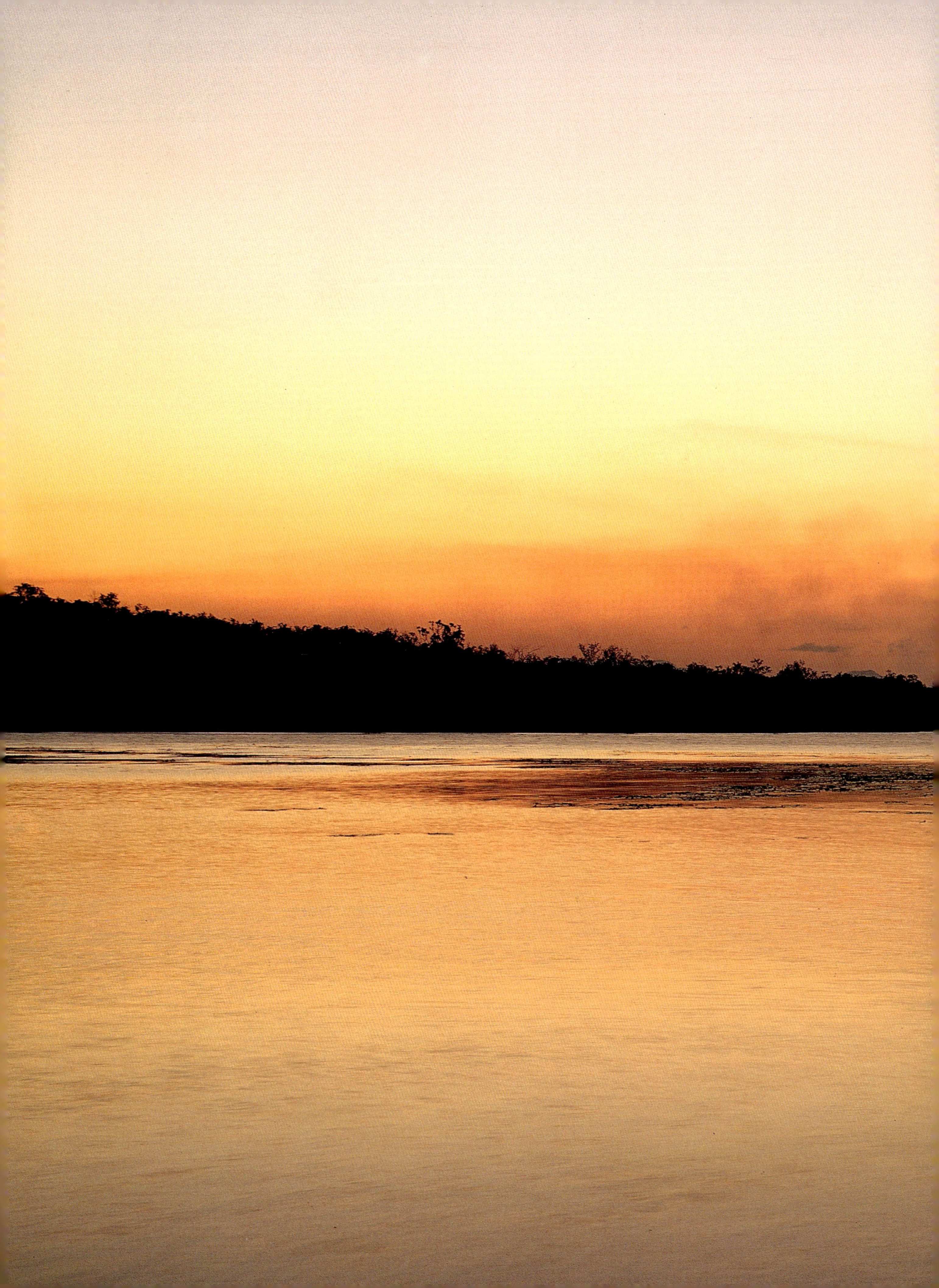

THE CENTRAL COAST
Harvesting nature's bounty and island hopping

They call the area around Mackay 'the natural north' and sophistication is certainly not the key word here. There is, however, a quiet charm about this region where the first European settlers found an ideal climate for growing the sugar cane which soon became one of Queensland's key industries.

Mackay is not the best-known name on the tourist route, and this is perhaps the source of its appeal. The hotels here may not be five-star but the islands are among some of the finest on the Barrier Reef. A trip to Bushy Atoll in a seaplane provides one of the best opportunities to see the full glory of a coral garden in a cut-off lagoon far from the tourist hordes. Mackay is also the jumping-off point for the renowned waterways of the Whitsunday Islands, and one- or five-day cruises operate out of Mackay for those who don't want to do their own sailing.

Mackay has three excellent beaches close to the city centre. Further afield, it's possible to buy fresh local mangoes and pawpaws from stalls on Bucasia Beach and Blacks Beach, while the dining room of the Pacific Hotel at Eimeo must have the best view of any pub in the world.

One of the region's most exciting natural areas is Eungella National Park, an hour's drive inland. The road undulates through sleepy country towns past huge sugar mills and country pubs that haven't changed in 100 years, up into the 50 000-hectare rainforest where visitors have their best chance of seeing that shy marsupial, the platypus, in the wild. At Broken River, inside the Park, as many as eight or nine of these creatures that so puzzled the early European explorers come out of their underwater burrows just before dawn and after sunset to swim and dive and frolic in the golden waters of the river.

opposite: Whitehaven Beach encapsulates the popular image of a tropical paradise.
previous pages: Sunset over the tranquil waters of Kinchant Dam, Mackay.

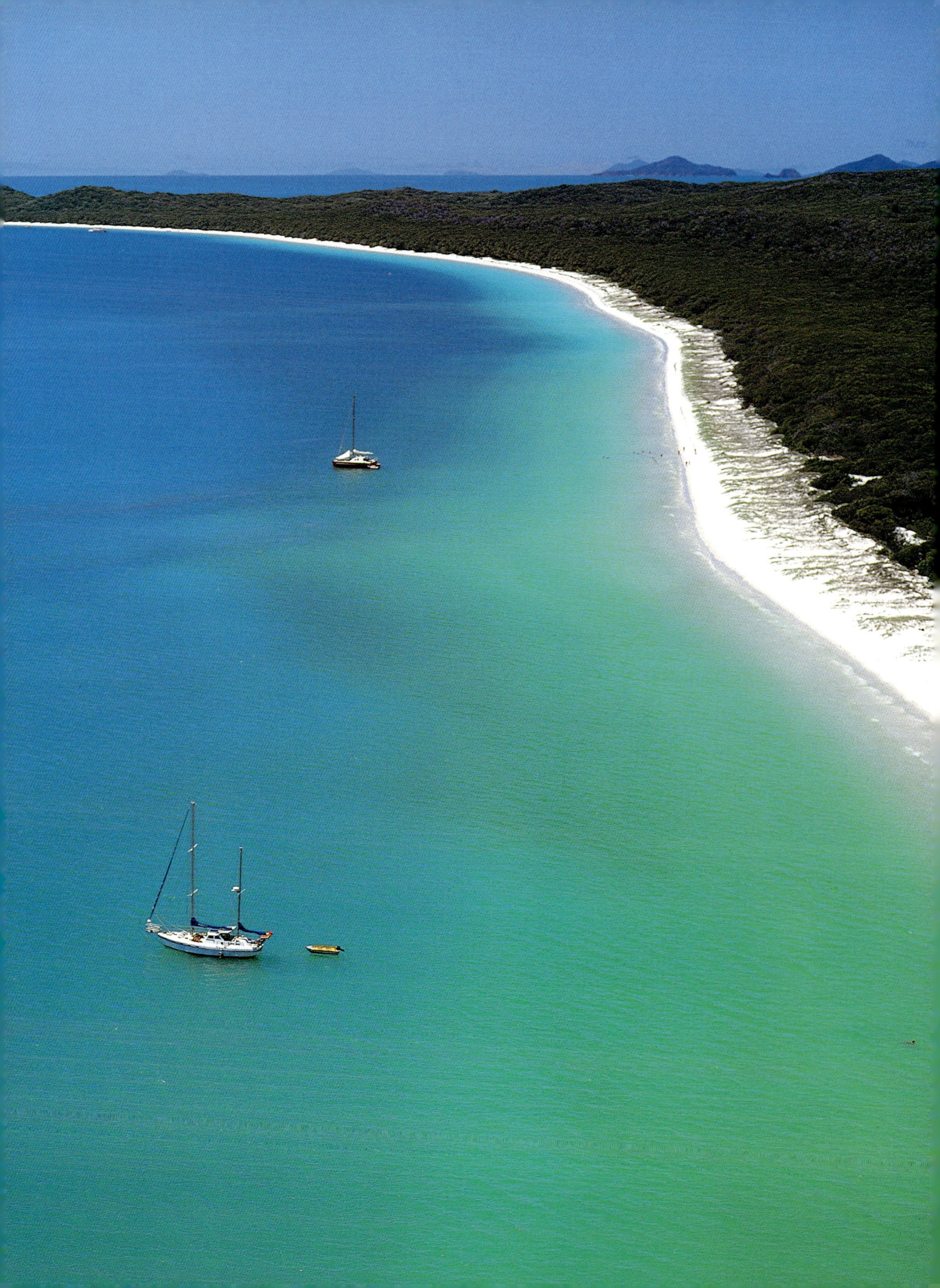

THE CENTRAL COAST - *Shute Harbour and Airlie Beach*

Shute Harbour and Airlie Beach - THE CENTRAL COAST

left: These fishing enthusiasts at popular Airlie Beach can be assured of a splendid haul of bream and flathead today.

opposite top: Small pleasure boats make their way into the safety of Shute Harbour after a truly glorious day cruising around the spectacular Whitsundays.

top: At Airlie Beach, swimmers in an enclosed ocean pool are well protected from encountering the deadly box jellyfish.

above: The windsurfer or the catamaran? That's the only decision these sun-lovers need to make on another perfect sailing day at tropical Airlie Beach.

THE CENTRAL COAST - *Hayman Island*

right: Pale pink puffs of soft coral stand out against royal blue waters so clear tiny fish seem suspended in midair. While corals like this one can be found in all reef habitats, they achieve their most spectacular forms in the deeper areas.

below: A lone yacht towing a dinghy in its wake slips through a glistening aquamarine sea. Escaping the tourist crowd is easy when you have access to a boat like this one, and the Whitsunday region is the 'charter yacht capital' of Australia.

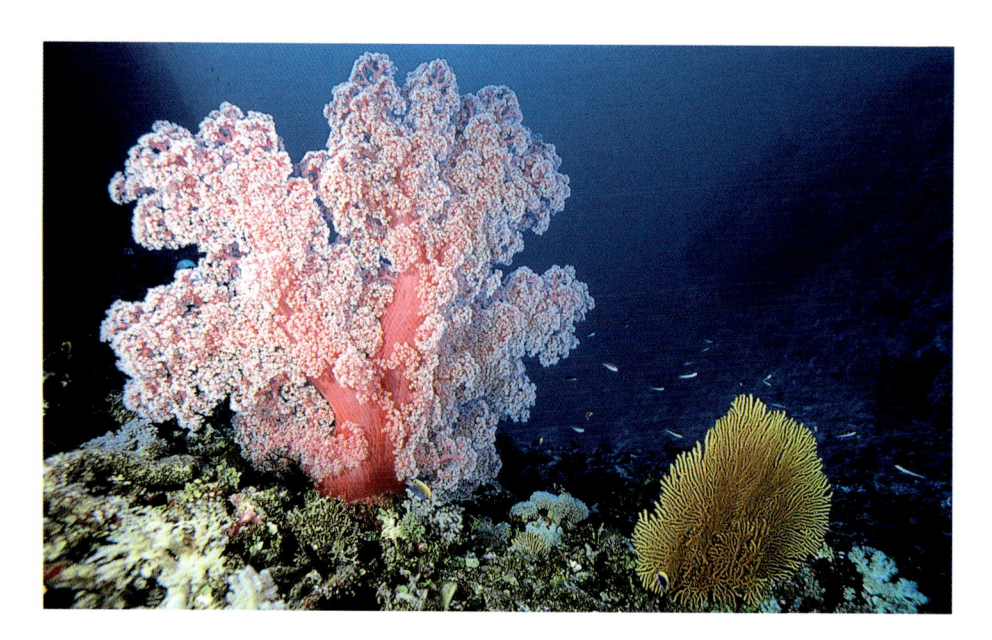

Whitsundays and Whitehaven - THE CENTRAL COAST

above: Like tiny jewels in the ocean, two of the hundred or so islands that make up the Whitsunday group glisten in the sparkling sunlight.

following pages: Never was a place more appropriately named. The sand sweeps gloriously into the inlet of Whitehaven Beach like snow on a winter day.

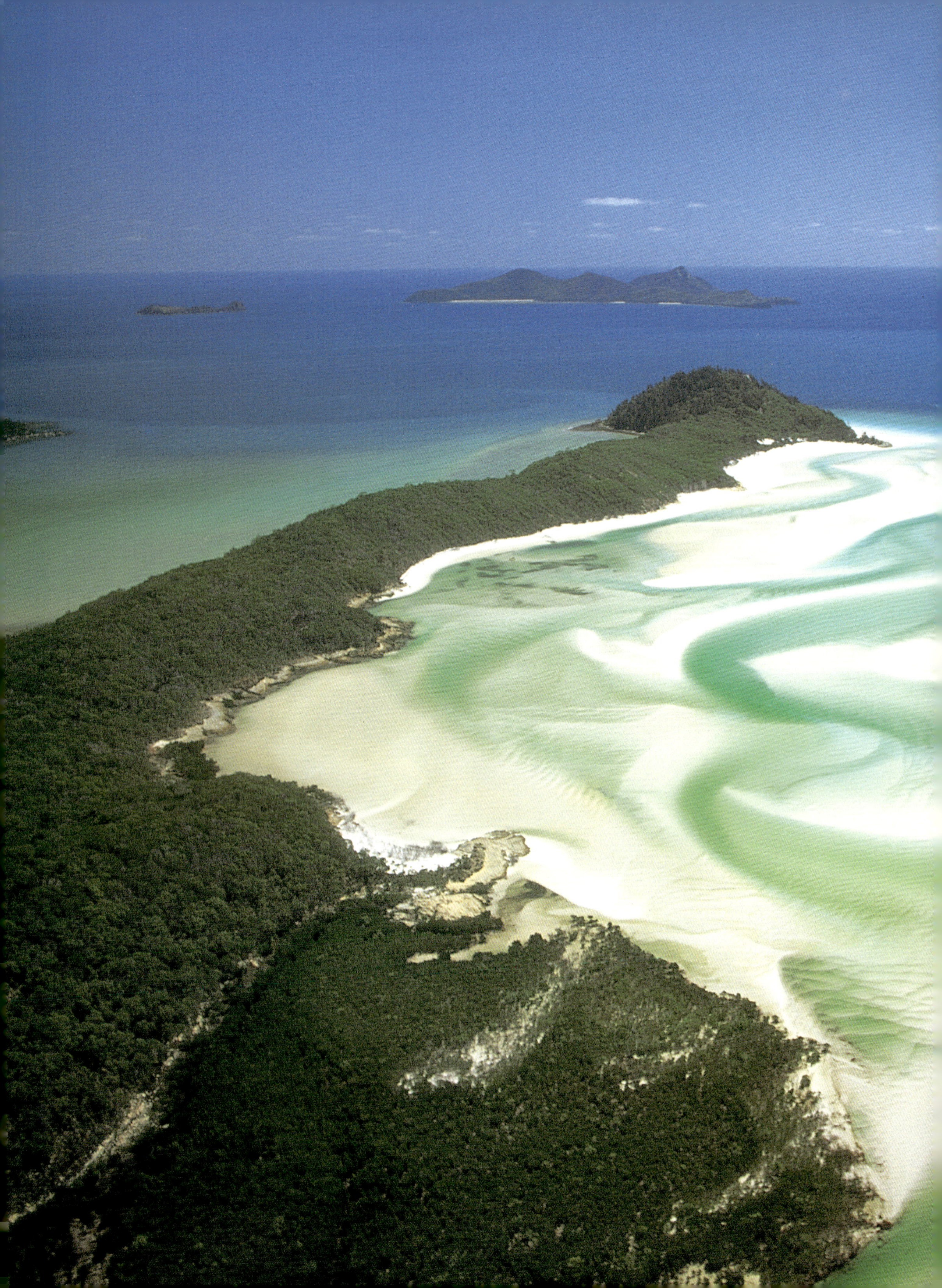

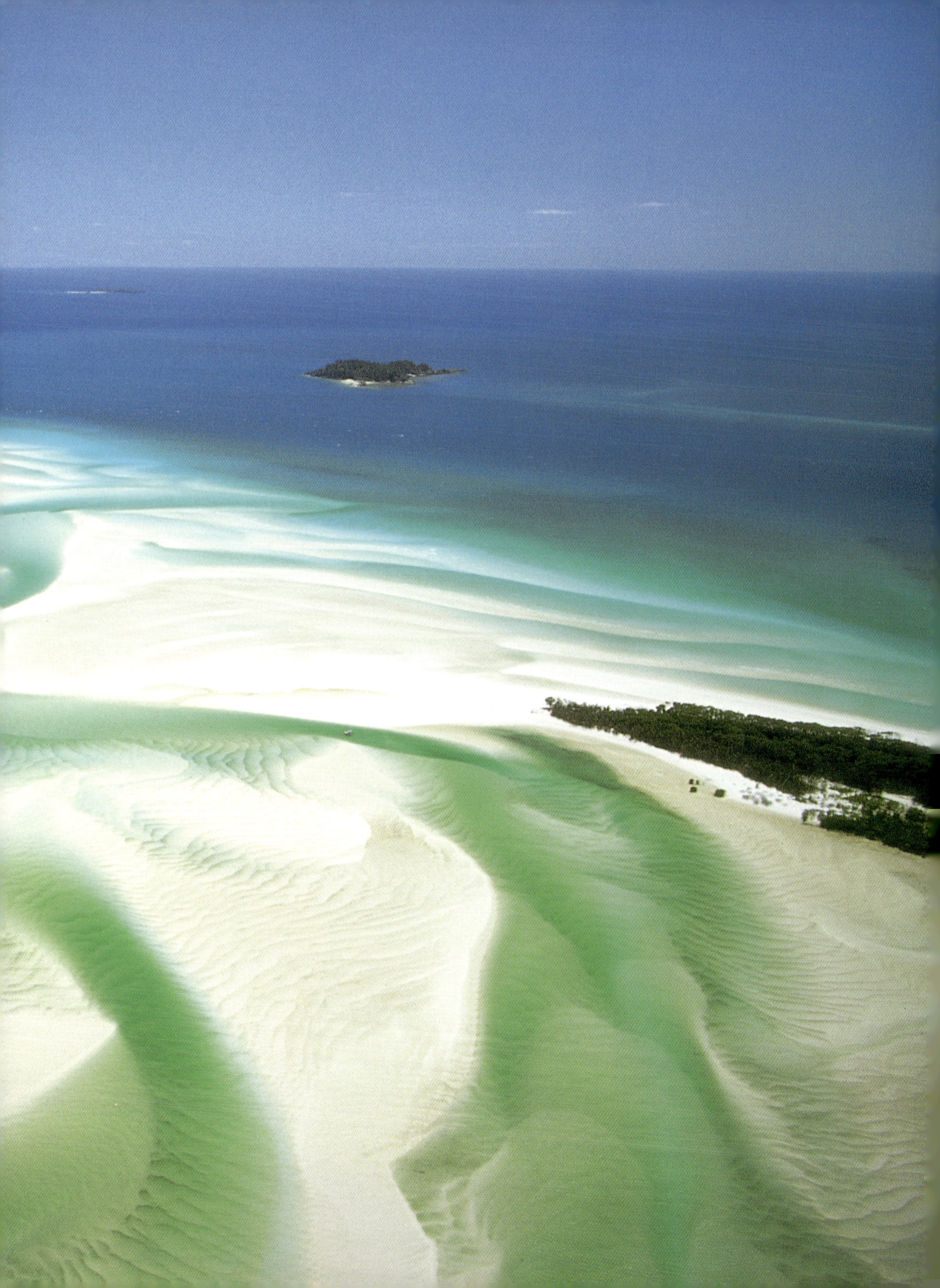

THE CENTRAL COAST - *Hook and Daydream Islands*

Hook and Daydream islands - THE CENTRAL COAST

above: The calm clear waters of the Whitsunday Passage make it ideal for watersports of all kinds. Here a jet skier gets right away from the crowds.

top: Daydream Island, one of the oldest resorts in the Whitsunday group, is a favourite for family holidays. Day tours from the mainland also stop here regularly.

left: The ripples of the Whitsunday Passage serve to enhance the reflection of idyllic Hook Island, with its fine sand and lush vegetation, in the clear water.

THE CENTRAL COAST - *South Molle Island*

above: During summer, flowering poinsettia trees attract hundreds of rainbow lorikeets. These birds are among Queensland's many varieties of raucous multicoloured parrots.

top: Parasailing is another popular sport in the Whitsundays. Fun in the sun takes on a whole new meaning in the skies above South Molle Island.

right: Colourful grasses on South Molle Island provide a vivid contrast to the more subtle blue and green nuances in this natural symphony of forest, sky and ocean.

South Molle Island - THE CENTRAL COAST

THE CENTRAL COAST - *Hamilton Island*

Hamilton Island - THE CENTRAL COAST

opposite: From the bustling resort of Hamilton Island, visitors can escape into long peaceful days on the water, where nothing matters but sea and sky.

above: The highly sophisticated Hamilton Island resort has a jet airport and accommodation ranging from Polynesian bures to high-rise apartments.

following pages: Anemonefish like these colourful specimens have little fear of human beings and are commonly seen by snorkellers in the waters of the Reef.

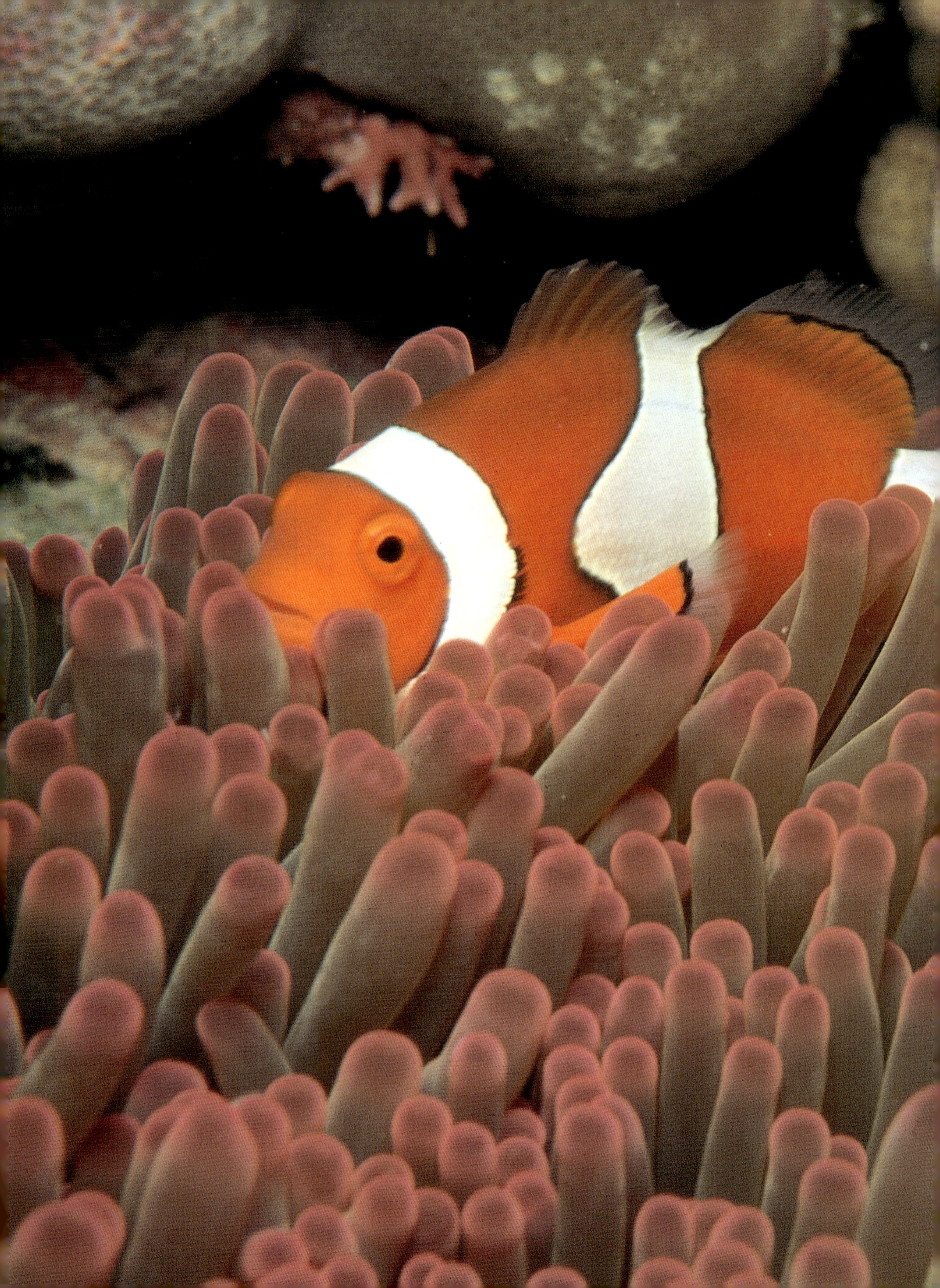

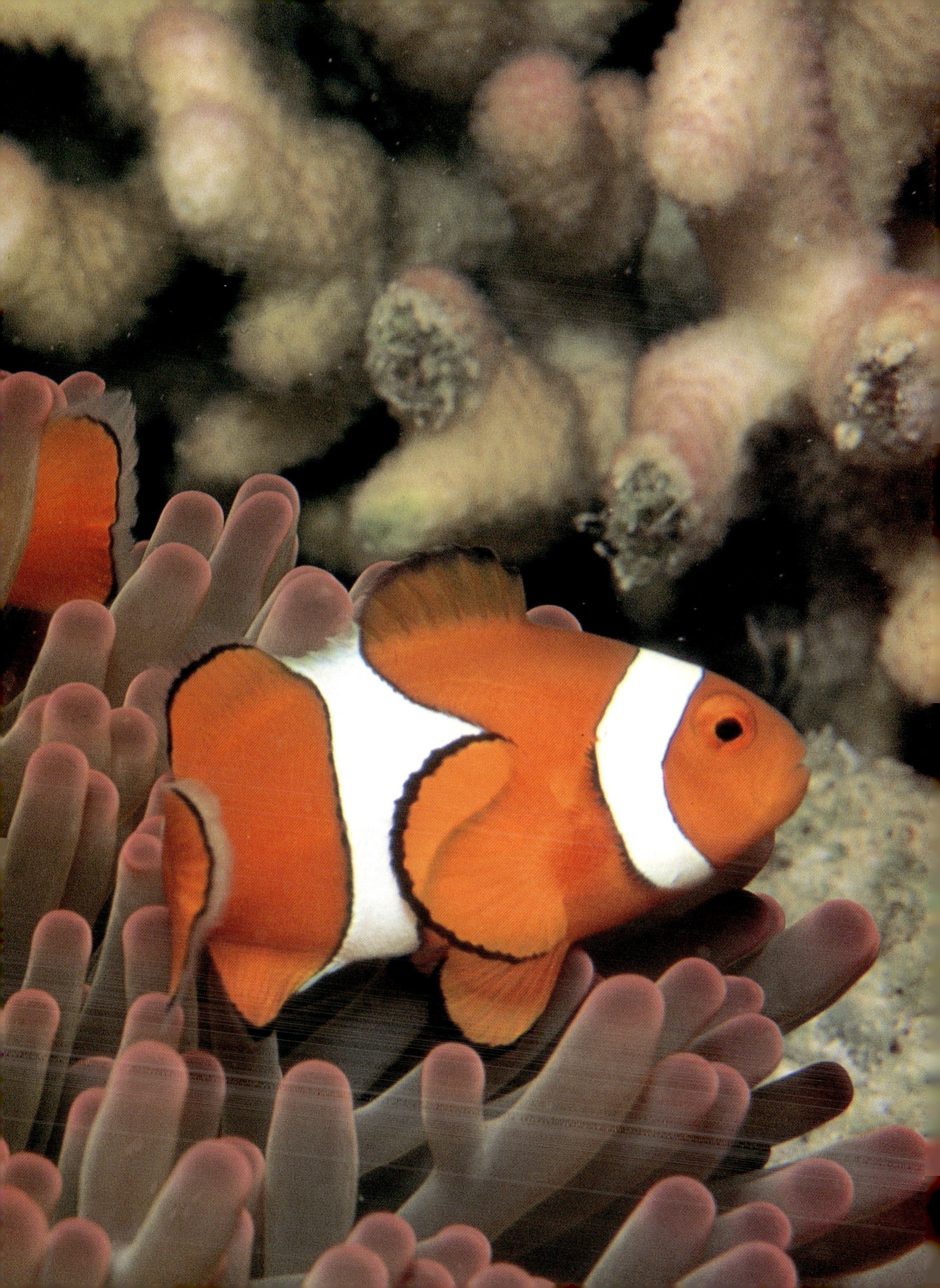

THE CENTRAL COAST - *Lindeman Island*

Lindeman Island - THE CENTRAL COAST

opposite: A Club Med Resort Village, recently opened on Lindeman Island, allows visitors to enjoy all the activities of a resort lifestyle. The rest of the island, however, remains untouched national park.

above: Sharks, stonefish, marine stingers, or coral cuts pose no threat for swimmers in Club Med's luxurious pool. The resort retains the atmosphere of the tropics while providing sheltered swimming.

left: Far away from the crowds at Lindeman's Club Med, it's possible to take in the subtle beauty of a tropical sunrise from the magnificent solitude of Mount Oldfield, the highest point in the national park which still covers most of the island. A graded bush track leads up to the summit.

THE CENTRAL COAST - *Southern Whitsundays*

Southern Whitsundays - THE CENTRAL COAST

opposite: Daytrippers and resort guests alike can experience the beauty of a tropical sunset on Brampton Island.

above: In a living palette of tropical sea colours, rich cream melts from pure white into the deepest green.

THE CENTRAL COAST - *Outer Reef*

above: Even non-swimmers can explore the mysterious underwater world from the comfort of this semi-submersible, where passengers sit below the waterline to view the reef in comfort.

right: What else would it be called but Heart Reef? This little gem is a typical example of a tiny cay created by living coral, not yet established enough to support vegetation.

Mackay and Eungella - THE CENTRAL COAST

above: Mackay is sometimes known as the 'sugar capital' of Australia, not surprising since the sugar mills of the district process a third of Australia's total sugar cane crop.

THE CENTRAL COAST - *Mackay and Eungella*

above: The national park at Eungella (an Aboriginal word meaning 'land of clouds') contains deep gorges sheltering a multitude of palms and ferns. There is a major platypus habitat in the rainforest here, with a special viewing platform at Broken River.

right: Half an hour south-west of Mackay is an undercover orchid conservatory, where rare blooms like these grow with other tropical plants in a rainforest environment complete with waterfalls and pools stocked with tropical fish.

opposite top: Experienced snorkellers and beachcombers agree that some of the best coral and marine life on the Reef is to be found at Bushy Atoll, accessible only by boat or by half-day seaplane excursions from Mackay.

opposite bottom: Soft corals like this Gorgonian fan lack the rigid limestone skeletons of hard corals. Under ideal conditions, where currents are periodically strong, sea fans can grow to over three metres in diameter.

Bushy Atoll - THE CENTRAL COAST

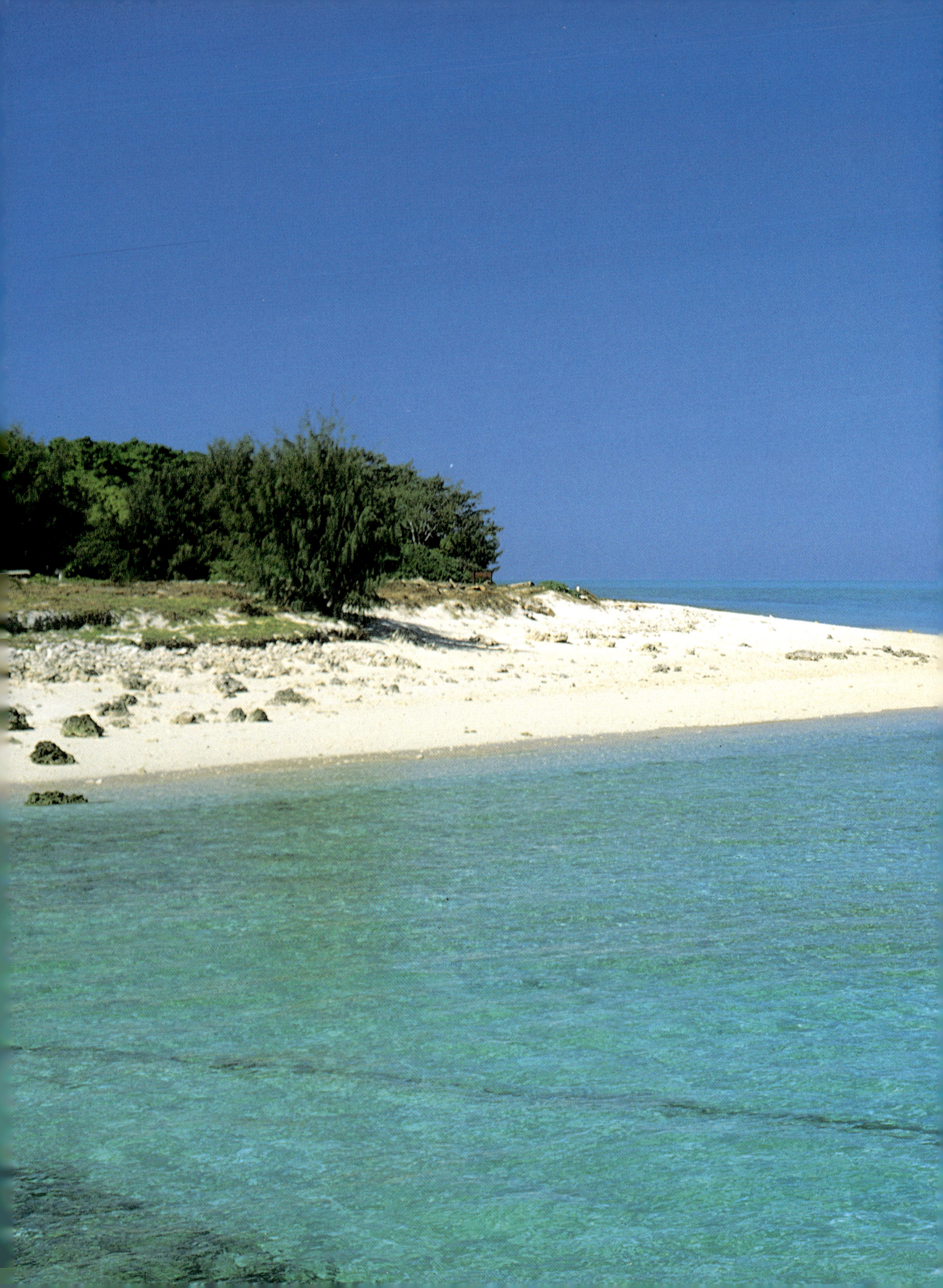

THE SOUTHERN REEF
Coral cays, sugar cane, manta rays and beef

$\mathcal{T}$he southern part of the Great Barrier Reef stretches from Rockhampton on the Tropic of Capricorn to the sugar town of Bundaberg in the south, and because it lies in the subtropics, it usually escapes the monsoon rains that can sometimes put a dampener on a holiday in the wet tropics. On islands like Heron and Lady Elliot the weather is almost guaranteed to be perfect; there was a time when guests at these resorts were offered another holiday free if they were rained out three days in a row.

Rockhampton proudly boasts of being the beef capital of Australia, and the steaks in the many restaurants have been known to defeat even the heartiest appetite. But there is more to do around here than merely eat, for some of Queensland's most outstanding tourist attractions are within easy striking distance of the town. Just a few minutes to the north are limestone caves where visitors can either take a guided tour or wander at their own pace through the spectacular underground caverns, some of which are home to hundreds of bentwing bats. The Koorana Crocodile Farm is another popular attraction.

North of the city, just outside Yeppoon, 10 000 sprawling hectares of wetlands form part of the Capricorn International Resort where you don't have to be a guest at one of the three hotels in the complex to see the biggest variety of waterfowl in Australia outside Kakadu National Park.

Further south, on the southern reef, the resort islands of Heron and Lady Elliot attract divers from all over the world to unsurpassed scuba diving and snorkelling in clear, safe, unpolluted waters. These islands, along with Mon Repos on the mainland, are also the best places to see the giant turtles come ashore and lay their eggs between November and February each year.

opposite: Only native Australian plants are grown in Gladstone's botanic gardens.
previous pages: These dive boats are at anchor off tiny Heron Island, known as 'just a drop in the ocean'.

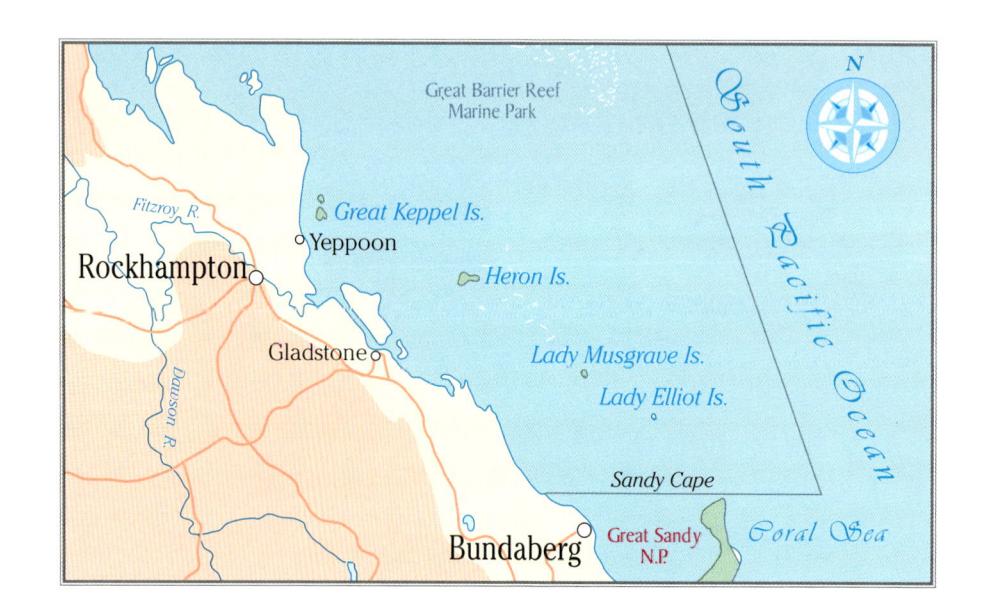

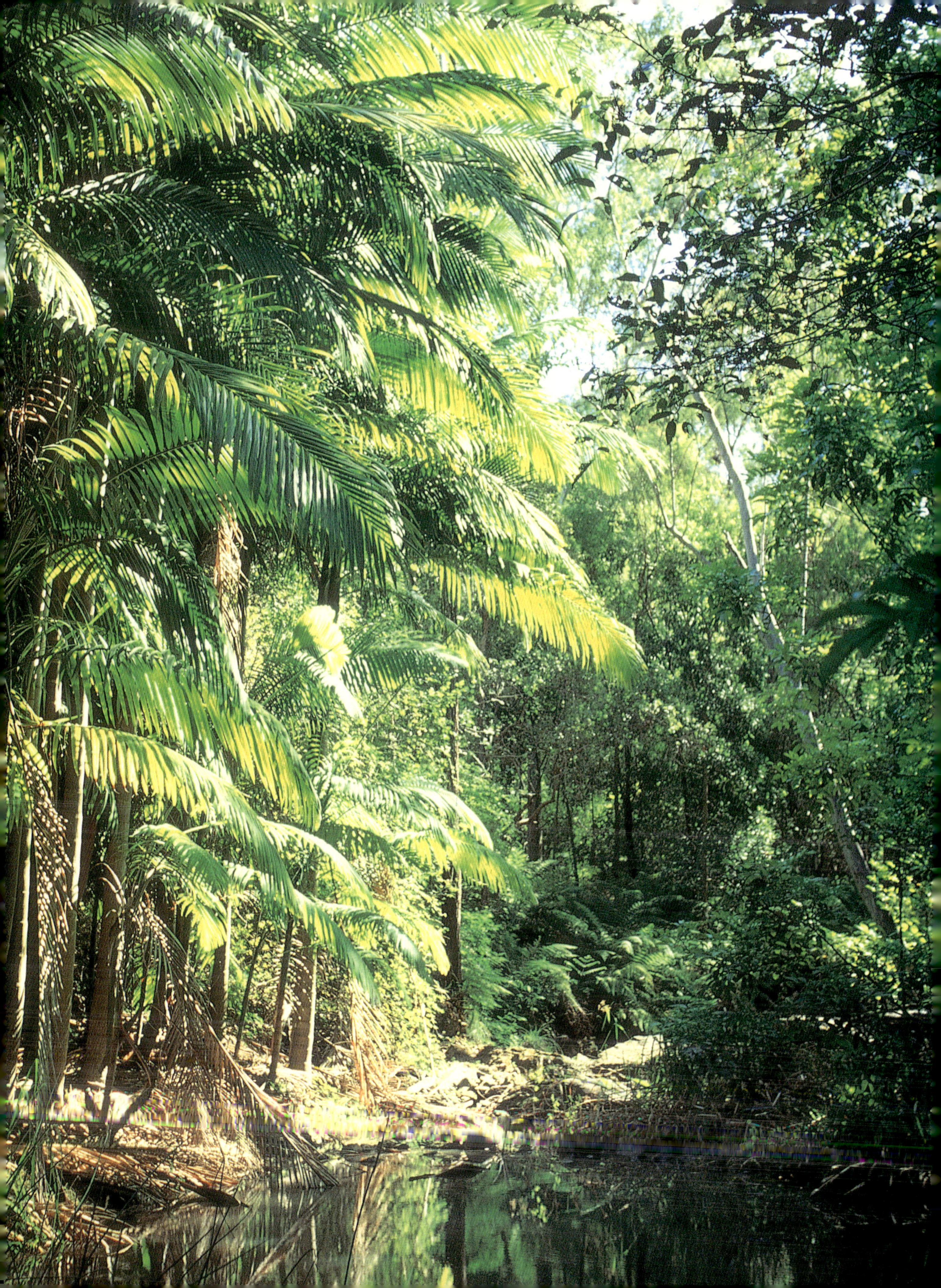

THE SOUTHERN REEF - *Rockhampton*

above: A face that only a mother could love. This crocodile hatchling could finish up on the dining table, as a handbag, or as another fearsome specimen at Rockhampton's Koorana Crocodile Farm.

opposite top: Not many caves occur above ground, but Olsens Caverns are inside a hill formed from an ancient coral reef. Opened to the public in 1884, they are Queensland's oldest tourist attraction.

opposite bottom: Situated right on the Tropic of Capricorn, Rockhampton straddles the subtropics and the tropics. Feeding time for the animals in the extensive Botanic Gardens and Zoo is at 3pm.

Rockhampton - THE SOUTHERN REEF

THE SOUTHERN REEF - *Yeppoon*

Yeppoon - THE SOUTHERN REEF

opposite bottom: Lammermoor Beach, one of many stretches of almost deserted coastline near Yeppoon, is the ideal place to enjoy a spectacular sunrise.

top left: The Capricorn International Resort at Yeppoon has two international-standard golf courses. It also boasts 22 kilometres of beachfront, and 8800 hectares of wetland wilderness teeming with native birds and animals.

top right: A scenic half-day trip south along the coast from Yeppoon leads to the rugged headland of Emu Park, with its famous Singing Ship sculpture. The wind blowing through this unique structure produces a variety of musical notes.

left: They claim it's the largest freshwater swimming pool in the Southern Hemisphere, and there's certainly room here for all the guests at the Capricorn International Resort

THE SOUTHERN REEF - Great Keppel

right: Great Keppel is known as the young people's island, mainly because of its superb beaches and its reasonably priced accommodation. And there's always the added attraction of a rubber duckie!

opposite top: Who needs a jetty when you can disembark from the Seafari at Great Keppel Island without getting your feet wet? Only 12 kilometres from the mainland at Yeppoon, the island's resort is serviced by fast cruise boats.

below: There couldn't be a more idyllic place in the world to get wrecked than on Great Keppel Island, with its long stretches of pure white sand and sapphire sea — especially when there's a modern resort just around the corner.

Great Keppel - THE SOUTHERN REEF

THE SOUTHERN REEF - Heron Island

right: The white heron is the symbol of tiny Heron Island, but the majestic bird has to compete with thousands of mutton-birds and noddies that congregate here in the nesting season.

below: Heron Island, a tiny coral cay with a scientific research station and a small resort, is part of the Reef itself. It is renowned for its easy access to some of the world's best snorkelling.

Heron Island - THE SOUTHERN REEF

above: Reef walking with a trained guide is one of the best ways of learning the wonders of the Great Barrier Reef. The Heron Island resort conducts reef walks every day at low tide.

right: During the nesting season, between November and March, hundreds of female turtles come ashore at night to lay their clutches of eggs in shallow nests in the sand. Heron Island is one of the world's most important green turtle rookeries.

following pages: Although Heron Island is only 16 hectares in area, there are still long stretches of deserted beach where pure white coral sand gleams through the clear unpolluted waters of the South Pacific.

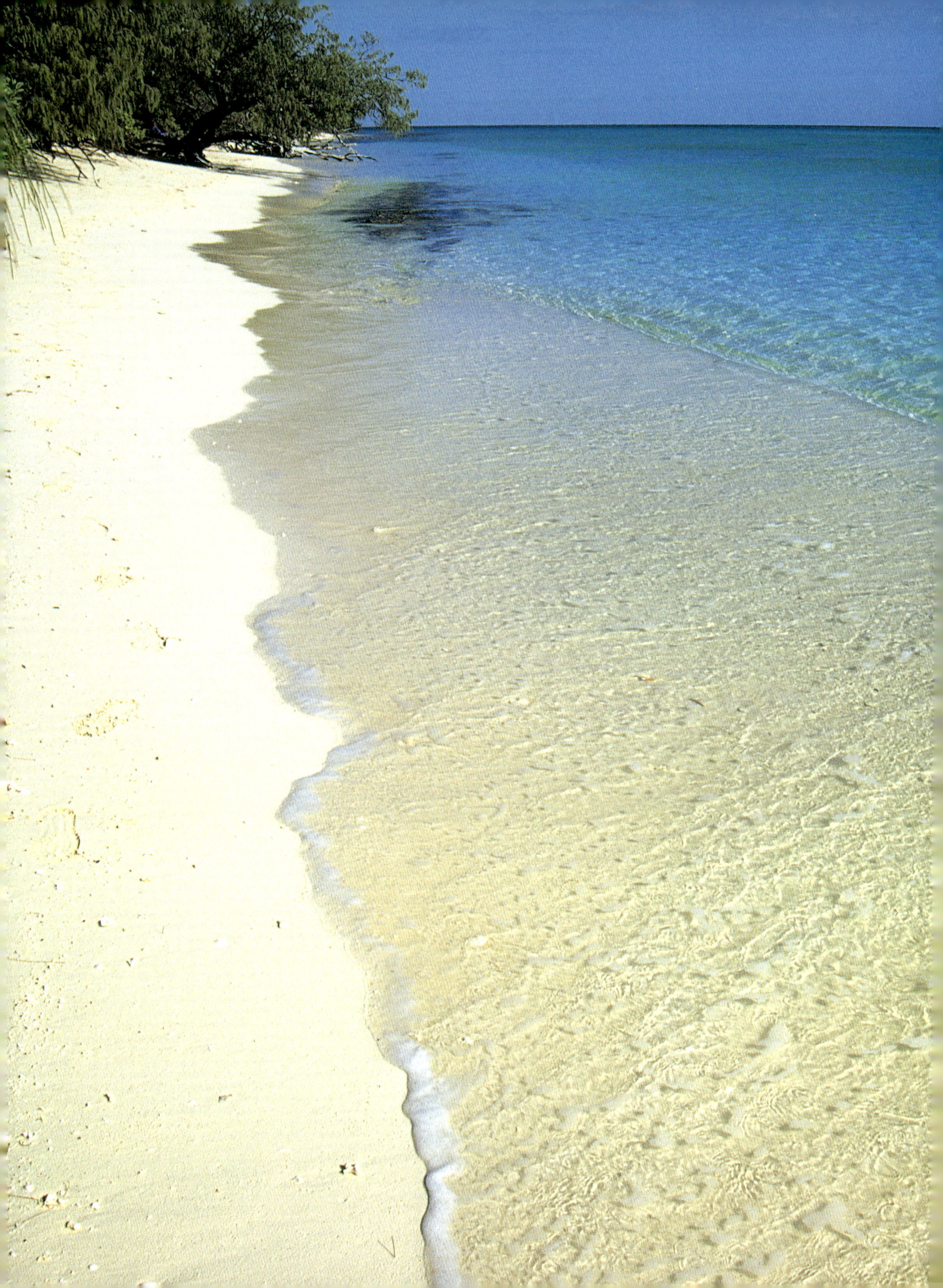

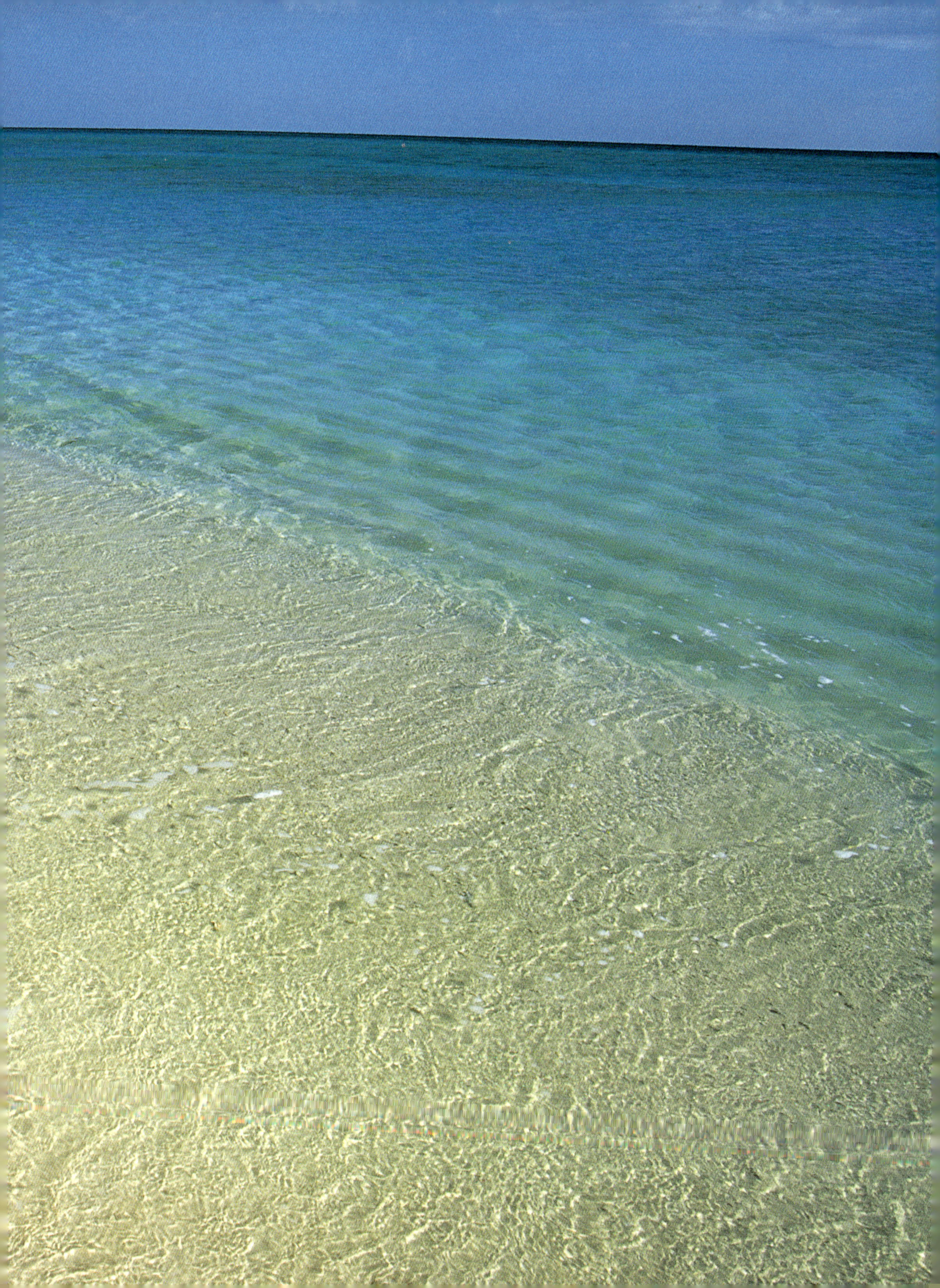

THE SOUTHERN REEF - *Gladstone and environs*

Gladstone and environs - THE SOUTHERN REEF

above: Camping holidays provide an opportunity to experience pioneer life in Queensland's awe-inspiring bushland. Access to camping sites on the banks of the Calliope River, inland from Gladstone, is restricted to four-wheel-drive vehicles, thus ensuring that the tranquil beauty of the area is not disturbed by too many tourists.

left: Gladstone, a modern city of 25 000 people, is a major seaport as well as the home of the Queensland Alumina Refinery. A local fisherman displays his catch of Moreton Bay Bugs, king prawns, reef fish and, of course, the famous Queensland Muddie (or mud crab) to an eager group of gourmets.

opposite bottom: The town of Seventeen-Seventy claims to be the birthplace of Queensland, for it was here that Captain Cook first set foot on the part of the country that a hundred years later became Australia's second-largest state. The rugged beauty of Round Hill, overlooking Bustard Bay, has changed little since those times.

THE SOUTHERN REEF - *Bundaberg*

above: The rich soil around Bundaberg makes it ideal for agriculture. The patchwork landscape of these canefields produces one-fifth of Australia's sugar, which is also processed into syrup, treacle and molasses.

top: On a windswept hillside, the skeletons of old gum trees stand watch over the town of Bundaberg, known for its agricultural produce, extensive sugar plantations and the world-famous Bundy Rum.

Lady Elliot Island - THE SOUTHERN REEF

above: A giant ray drifts past Lady Elliot Island, the southernmost island of the Reef. This coral cay is famous for its manta rays, also known as devilfish, and for its wide variety of fish life.

THE SOUTHERN REEF - *Lady Elliot Island*

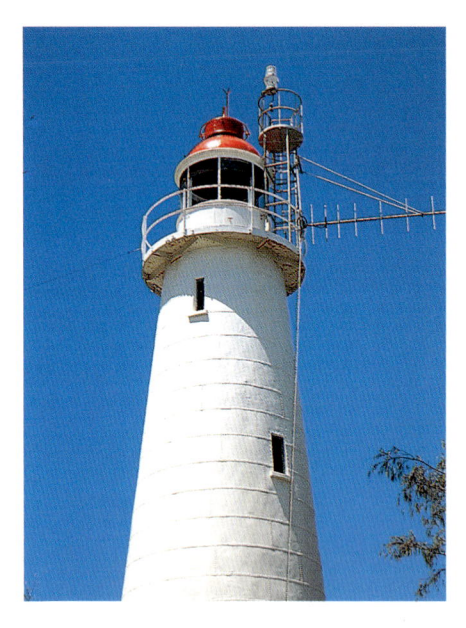

above: The lighthouse at Lady Elliot Island dates back to 1866, but like all lighthouses on the Queensland coast these days, it is now fully mechanised.

top: Thousands of mutton-birds nest on the ground at Lady Elliot Island, and visitors soon begin to wish the noisy chicks would grow up and fly away.

right: Snorkelling in the clear waters of Lady Elliot Island is a rewarding experience. Other pleasures include reef walking, scuba diving and glass-bottomed boats.

Lady Elliot Island - THE SOUTHERN REEF

INDEX

Aboriginal
  culture, 44, 45, 76
  early settlement, 14–15
accommodation, 13, 38–39
Airlie Beach, 25, 119
Atherton Tableland, 76, 78, 82

beaches, 22, 25, 63, 116
Bedarra Island, 21, 93
Billabong Sanctuary, 96
birdlife, 25, 34, 142
blue-ringed octopus, 31
boating, 41
Bowan, 96
Brampton Island, 25, 135
Broken River, 116
Bucasia Beach, 116
Bundaberg, 25, 156
Bushy Atoll, 24, 25, 138

Cairns, 25, 44, 70–73
Calliope River, 155
camping, 25, 39, 155
Cape Tribulation, 25, 36, 48, 59
Cape York, 48, 51
Cape York Peninsula, 19
Charters Towers, 96
Chillagoe National Park, 79, 82
climate, 18
Cook, Captain James, 13, 14, 15, 18, 23, 155
Cooktown, 48, 57
coral, 17, 26–28, 31
  destruction, 16
coral cays, 25
coral islands, 18
Coral Sea, 48
crocodiles, 37
crustaceans, 30

Daintree River, 48, 60
dangerous creatures, 31
Daydream Island, 23
daytripping, 25
diving, 21, 25, 41–42
dolphins, 32, 102
Dreamtime Cultural Centre, 44

dugongs, 32
Dunk Island, 13, 16, 21, 89, 92

echinoderms, 28
ecosystem, protection of, 16, 37, 99
eco-tourism, 38
Edward River Crocodile Farm, 44
Elinjaa Falls, 82
Emu Park, 147
Eungella National Park, 116, 138
European settlement, 15–16

fish, 29, 31, 98
fishing, 25, 40
formation, 17

Gladstone, 25
goldmining towns, 96
Great Barrier Reef Marine Park, 16
Great Barrier Reef Wonderland, 45, 96
Great Keppel Island, 25, 148
Green Island, 20, 75

Hamilton Island, 23, 129
Hardy's Reef, 13
Hayman Island, 23
Heart Reef, 136
Hergert Bay, 99
Heron Island, 25, 30, 142, 150, 151
Hinchinbrook Island, 21–22, 99
holiday activities, 13, 20, 22, 25, 38–45

Ingham, 103
Innisfail, 85

jellyfish, 31

koalas, 22
Koorana Crocodile Farm, 44, 142, 144
Kuranda, 44, 45, 76

Lady Elliot Island, 17, 20, 25, 30, 142, 157, 158
Lake Barrine, 82
Lammermoor Beach, 147
landsports, 43
life forms, 17
Lindeman Island, 23, 133
Lizard Island, 15, 20, 48
location, 13
Long Island, 23

Mackay, 25, 116, 137
Magnetic Island, 18, 22–23, 96, 106
mammals, 32
marine life, 17
Michaelmas Cay, 21, 66
Millaa Millaa, 82
Mission Beach, 87
Missionary Bay, 21, 22
molluscs, 28
Mon Repos, 30
Mossman Gorge, 62
Mossman River, 48
Mount Spec National Park, 44, 103
Muggy Muggy Beach, 89

Nelly Bay, 18

Olsens Caverns, 144
Orpheus Island, 102

Palm Bay, 23
Palm Cove, 48, 67
Palm Islands, 22
parasailing, 126
platypus, 116
Port Douglas, 25, 63

rainfall, 18
rainforest, 25, 35, 36–37
Ravenswood, 96
reef
  types, 18
  viewing, 42–43
  walking, 151
Rockhampton, 44, 142

sharks, 31
shells, 28, 31

shipwrecks, 15
size, 17
Skyrail, 76
snakes, 31
snorkelling, 41–42
South Molle Island, 23, 126
steam train, 76
stingrays, 31

Thursday Island, 48
Tjapukai Aboriginal Cultural Park, 44, 45, 76
tourism
  development, 16
  effect, 16
Townsville, 25, 44, 96, 109
Tully River Gorge, 87
turtles, 30–31, 142, 151

Undara lava tubes, 98
Undine Cay, 12, 41

vegetation, 18, 34–35

Wallaman Falls, 103
watersports, 25, 43
Wet Tropics Management Authority, 37
whales, humpback, 18, 32
Whitehaven Beach, 121
whitewater rafting, 87
Whitsunday Islands, 23, 93, 120–121
Whitsunday Passage, 125
wildlife, 25, 37, 44–45
World Heritage listing, 16, 17, 36

yachting, 23
Yeppoon, 25, 142, 147

Zillie Falls, 82
Zoe Bay, 99